The Digital DJ Handbook

10 Steps To A
Successful
DJ Business

By Karl Wiebe

Copyright © 2013 Karl Wiebe

All rights reserved.

ISBN: 1481928384

ISBN-13: 978-1481928380

The Digital DJ Handbook

Karl Wiebe

TABLE OF CONTENTS

Introduction

We've all seen it. The party is rocking and everyone is up on the dance floor. The wedding (or any other party) is in full swing... the lights are low and the drinks are flowing, the music is pumping and the food tastes great. Even grandma is up on the dance floor. Smiles are everywhere. It is truly a night to remember.

You spot some friends from across the busy room—hey look who's arrived!

"Let's dance!"

"I love this song!"

"I haven't heard this one in ages!"

"I'm fourteen years old again!"

Everyone is into it—the night is magical.

Suddenly, the DJ switches the music and the entire atmosphere changes. He went from a great medley of rock songs that everyone instantly recognized and loved to a couple of obscure sleeper tracks that no one has ever heard of. And what was that? An R&B dance groove? Did the song just blast a swear word? I've never heard of this song before. Oh well... there are confused glances, the dance floor clears, people run off to the bathroom, and a few people sneak outside for a cigarette.

The DJ at any party has huge power. Simply put, they can make or break an event. Either way, however, at the end of the night, the DJ gets paid and gets paid well. If the event is a flop, the DJ can take some heat and be the recipient of untold grief and stress.

If the above scenario has you excited and ready to "be the man" behind the microphone, this book is for you.

Why should you read this book? I hope that you are interested in starting up and running a successful DJ business. By "successful", I mean both profitable and enjoyable. The best "work" in life is not really work at all. It is doing what you enjoy and getting paid for it. There are lots of things that you can do in your spare time, and many different business ventures. First and foremost, we want to have fun, but it is imperative that we get paid (and paid well). After all, this is a business, not just a hobby.

DJing a party or a dance can be extremely fun and financially and emotionally rewarding—under the right circumstances. It can also be a huge headache and much more work than necessary if the proper preparation and time is not spent working on the important details of your business. How would you like to prepare for hours, travel through rough winter weather to some obscure golf clubhouse outside of town and then spend an evening surrounded by grumpy, tired, stressed-out people who don't like your music? Asking for money at the end of such an evening does not make it any less stressful—in fact it might only add to it!

Many people in the business will tell you that being a DJ is hard work and that the business of entertaining hundreds of people at a wedding, party of other important event is technically complicated. But the real fact of life is that the DJ business, like most businesses out there, are very simple. (I said simple—not easy.) As an entrepreneur, you are providing a service that others are willing to pay you money for. If you can be reliable and professional, show up on time, be energetic and polite, and be willing to do just a little bit more for your customer, word will get around and your business will thrive in the long run.

Sounds simple, doesn't it? The truth is that many businesses fail within the first five years. Very few last a long time. Go grab an old Yellow Pages telephone directory from a few years ago. See which restaurants, tailor shops and music stores are still in business just three to five years later. The phone books are filled with start-up businesses that disappear within the first couple of years. Why is this so? If DJing is so simple, why aren't there lots of DJ millionaires driving around in their Corvettes?

The fact of the matter is that there are many entrepreneurs walking around—DJs or otherwise. However, the majority of these business owners are not millionaires. There are many people who have small businesses on the side while they work full-time or part-time jobs. Many people already have careers—and some of them are well-paying careers. You might know a co-worker who works part-time and has a consulting trade on the side, be it in accounting, tax preparation or even construction. Lots of people have a "regular" job and then do something fun and profitable on the side, like on weekends or evenings.

Many full-time entrepreneurs fail at their dreams. We've all seen the small "mom and pop" shop close on the street corner. Why is this? A business—any business, in any industry—can fail due to a number of reasons. Examples include a poor business location (which means not enough customers for business), costs being too high (not making any actual profit) and burnout (working too hard and watching your family relationships and free time all crumble away). However, I started up a DJ business and made it work, and I have also teamed up with a local band who has been providing music professionally for the public for over two decades. I know that you can make it work too—all you need is some preparation, hard work and some professionalism. Do you have it in you?

I could quote a bunch of marketing experts and consultants, but that is not what this book is all about. Instead, I want to tell you about my experiences as a DJ over the last ten years. I have also included a couple of case studies at the back of the book—I hope that you find their insight helpful as well.

If you read every word of this book and love it, then great. Maybe there are a couple of select parts of the book that you find useful. That is fine too. Hopefully everyone who reads this book will find something rewarding for them, whether they are in a start-up band, a DJ service, or some other event planning business.

I found out about the DJ business when I was researching weddings in the mid-1990s. I found out about the exorbitant fees that a wedding DJ charged on a regular basis for very simple work. I had no idea that DJs made so much money and my eyes turned green. I spent about three years researching the DJ market and trying to learn about the technical and business-side of being a DJ. It was a long and frustrating experience. There aren't many really good books about being a DJ. Sure, there are a generic "starting up a business" books, but I had read those. Anytime I got near the specifics that I was looking for about being a DJ, the books suddenly veered away and said "check local businesses and opportunities" or "talk to local businesses". I was smart enough to know that walking into a local DJ store and asking them about their profit margin was probably not going to elicit a great response from the owner.

One good way to get experience as a DJ (according to the DJ books out there) is to work as a DJ for someone else. This is probably true. However, the money is not as good as if you are working for yourself. You will never get rich working for someone else, unless you happen to be a movie star or professional athlete. For the rest of us who aren't acting on television or throwing a hundred-mile-an-hour fastball, the road to wealth is paved with entrepreneur's ideas and hard work.

After having researched some local DJs in my city, my mouth watered when I thought about all the money we could make in the DJ business. How hard could it be to spin some tunes? Why were the DJ fees so expensive? Was it a hard business to get into? What sort of mistakes do most people starting out make? I learned through trial and error and some of my mistakes were costly both in dollars and stress. I will try to answer these and other questions throughout the book as they relate to our business, which I called Retro DJ.

Please note that this book was written for everyone looking to start a simple, profitable DJ business. It was written by me, a Canadian. I found that most DJ books out there were slanted towards the U.S. markets, but I wanted to create a handbook that was based on my experiences, which took place in Canada. However, this book has general enough tips for DJs all over the world, including the United States and other free-market countries. The basics are the same all over the world—after all, a rocking party is a great party, whether it is a community hall in Saskatchewan, a gymnasium in Iowa or a dance club in Mexico.

With the digital age upon us, there is an increasing concern about copyrights. We all have friends who burn CDs and get files and music from the internet. Is this legal? Just as important, is it ethical?

I try to answer some of these questions, or at least shed some light on them, by discussing the role of SOCAN (The Society of Composers, Authors and Music Publishers of Canada). This non-profit organization represents artists. But how does the whole industry operate? How complicated is it? In the United States, there is a company called ASCAP. If you have fears of playing "Stairway To Heaven" at a school dance and suddenly the police bust down the door, you are not alone. We'll take a look at copyright fears and concerns. Hopefully we can answer these questions and more. There is a great feeling associated with working hard and earning great sums of money honestly, and this book will help show you how to do exactly that.

The digital landscape has dramatically changed over the past five years. There is an increased popularity of Apple products (iPod, iPad, iTunes, etc). The sophistication of laptop computers and notebooks has also significantly increased, while the costs continue to call. The days of dragging a desktop computer to a DJ gig are long gone—the software now driving the mixer and speakers are held in tiny notebook computers or even a phone. While the technology is constantly evolving and improving, the basic mechanics of DJing has stayed the same—being a primary "reader" of the room and spinning tunes that will keep people interested, excited and happy. This is the real skill to being a DJ, whether you are using a clunky desktop computer, a laptop, or a tiny phone.

There are ten chapters in this book that represent "ten steps to success". Each chapter can be read individually, or from start to finish. I recommend reading the whole book through one time, and then revisiting chapters and making notes where appropriate. Remember, each DJ business is unique and only you can determine what are the important aspects of your business that require the most attention.

Let's explore the world of the digital DJ and have some fun!

Chapter 1:
Setting Up Your DJ Business

The first question that most people wonder about with DJing is "what's the big deal?" How hard can it be to spin some tunes? I take this as a great compliment. That means that we are making it look easy when we DJ an event. What people don't see are the time and energy involved in making any successful business work.

After I learned about the huge checks that are cashed by wedding DJs, I started thinking seriously about the DJ business. In the mid-1990s, the world was not fully digital the way it is now. As the 21st century has dawned, everything it would seem is online and in digital form. DJs no longer need to carry around boxes of tapes or a binder full of CDs. (Some still do however, because they either have the technology and / or the expertise to run this medium).

When we started up our DJ business, the goal was to have fun and make some money. That leads us to my first and most important rule: *have fun or don't do it*.

I have absolutely no doubt in my mind that there are some people out there who will scoff at this rule. "Come on, you mean to tell me that I must love what I'm doing in order to be successful?" My answer is yes. Yes! "What about all the garbage men and bus drivers out there? They are successful... who wants to be a garbage man?"

I stand by this rule more than any other in this book, which is why I put it first. If you look at any successful business person, they all have one thing in common: they love doing what they are doing. Using the garbage man example, you can argue that many people enjoy working with little or no supervision, they don't want to be in an office, they like driving, or they enjoy working outside. All of these things apply to being a garbage man. Some people love working with numbers. Marketing people often can't imagine being a happy accountant; finance people, on the other hand, shudder when they think about having to "make a sale" or entertain a client like sales people do all of the time. "People persons" thrive in an environment such as customer service or sales.

Are you introverted or extroverted? An introvert is a relatively quiet, shy or unassuming person. It doesn't necessarily mean you are boring—just that it may take a while to get to know you. An extrovert means that you are generally louder and more outgoing. Both types can be successful DJs, although you may find that extroverts will generally enjoy the experience more. Can you get up in front of two hundred people and talk into a microphone? Are you nervous just thinking about it? What about sitting up on stage, all night long, during a wedding or party? Sure, you can hide behind your laptop or speakers, but you will have to eventually talk to people, and lots of them.

What about talking to strangers on the phone? All sorts of people are going to call your business and ask you what type of services you provide, how much you charge, and if they can meet with you to discuss all sorts of details. Are you comfortable with that? If you have a website, that means that you are going to be fielding email requests. Many of these requests will not be serious—they will just be people who are costing out their wedding or party and are asking you about your services. How do you feel about working weekends—especially if you have had a long week, or are run down or not feeling particularly energetic? What if you have to cancel plans with your friends because you have a high-paying gig that you agreed to do? How well can you handle stress, and things that are out of your control?

Skills Every DJ Needs

You don't need to be a super-successful sales person or a slick advertising whiz to be a successful DJ. However, you do need some characteristics. I've listed them below.

- Professional
- Clean and groomed
- Able to drive a vehicle
- Polite
- Willing to listen to criticism
- Willing to listen to other ideas
- Enjoys talking to people, especially in public
- Willing to say no
- Punctual
- Sense of humor
- Able to handle pressure
- Willing to learn

Notice that I didn't put any advertising or accounting skills in there. This is because you can either learn to do those in your spare time, or, if you have no interest in those things, then you can pay someone to do those things for you. You can go to the local tax office and get your taxes done by someone who is truly passionate about filling out tax forms. You can go to a creative ad agency and run advertising that you may think is brilliant.

Similarly, you don't need to be particularly good with money. Many business books will spend time talking about money, marketing and accounting. Usually this type of talk scares off many entrepreneurs. "I don't have a business degree!" someone will usually moan. You can practically hear their dream shattering in the background. I won't spend your time with that stuff about accounting and money—we are here to get the music started and become a successful DJ! If you are not very good with money, then go to your local bank and talk with a consultant. You can usually set up a business account and then it's just a matter of physically going to the bank to deposit the cash or checks. Just be honest and tell them that you want a business account with low or no fees and shop around—go to a few banks and see if you can get a free or low-fee account.

That having been said, however, this book will deal with marketing. Marketing, which is the process of understanding your client's needs, is an integral part of your (and any) business.

It All Starts With Marketing

Marketing means researching your market. Before your start your business, you need to ask yourself some basic questions:

- Who are your customers going to be? School kids? Senior citizens? Weddings? Graduation parties?
- What type of music will you specialize in? Why? How knowledgeable are you about this type of music? Does anyone want to hear it?

- How much money are you willing to spend to advertise? (Don't be discouraged if this amount is extremely small to start.)

The best way to get a feel for the market for a DJ is to visit places that play music. Go out to the local pub or bar and pay attention to the music. Is there a wedding that you have been invited to? Make sure to get a table near the DJ for the evening and see how they set up and what types of music they play. If you are an outgoing person or if you get the feeling that the DJ is a nice or approachable person, go up to them and ask them how they are set up (for example, what type of speakers they use, why they chose the hardware that they did, etc.). Remember that they are working, so they might not want to spend an hour talking with you about how they are set up or why they are choosing to play Vanilla Ice at exactly 9:32 p.m. However, some DJs might be in "autopilot" mode for a short while during the event and have the time or the energy to discuss the business and what they like or don't like about it. One of the best way to gage enthusiasm for a conversation is to compliment the DJ and tell him why you liked something that they did (a song, hosting the party, etc.). If they are energetic and want to talk, ask a few questions and listen.

Is there a local community hall in your neighborhood or city? In some small towns, there might be one or two, but in large cities such as Calgary and Vancouver there are lots and they are everywhere. Check them out. See if there are posting at the halls for upcoming Halloween dances or community events and then go to them. See what the music is like. Start looking at events in the paper and attend them. In Calgary, for example, the Exhibition & Stampede runs every July for ten days. There is country music everywhere as many local businesses run stampede breakfasts and dinners. There's almost always a DJ in the background cranking out some country tunes and the public show up, eat pancakes and visit. Edmonton has the Klondike Days (now called "Edmonton's Capital EX", and Thunder Bay, Ontario has the CLE – The Canadian Lakehead Exhibition. Almost every city in Canada has festivities during Canada Day and Halloween. Every Saturday night there are bars all over the country that have music. Is there a market for your services?

This leads to a very important rule: *know about different styles of music*.

This doesn't mean that you have to be an expert in every style of music. However, you should know about different genres of music, including ones that you may not like.

I consider myself an expert in the classic rock genre. My business, called *Retro DJ*, specializes in rock n' roll from the 1950s through the 1980s. However, we quickly learned that the party was much more enjoyable when there was an occasional country song thrown in, or a current radio hit. At a wedding, for example, there are requests for waltzes and some really old "big band" hits on occasion. There are usually a higher percentage or senior citizens at a wedding than at another type of function, like a Halloween party for example. Know your audience and be prepared to play a little bit of different genres when the situation calls for it.

This, however, doesn't mean that you need to be a rap expert or have encyclopedic knowledge about R&B or big band at every event. When we DJ'd Calgary Stampede parties, for example, we never claimed to be the world's leading authority of country music. We basically bought the "greatest hits" packages that feature artists' big chart toppers and just played those for the evening with the occasional classic rock song that was "country" in flavor. (Specific songs and genres are discussed more in-depth in a later half of this book).

The Basics

So what exactly do you need to get started as a DJ? Here's the basic list.

- 2 professional speakers
- 1 mixer
- 1 microphone
- 1 microphone stand
- a good quality computer (or audio-playing device)
- power cords & music supplies (like batteries, a small lamp, etc.)
- a vehicle
- business cards
- A physical catalogue of songs that people can read

That's it. Remember, these are the basics. There are some other things that you could add in if you like, and those are discussed in the next section. This brings us to the rule concerning electronics: *buy high-quality hardware*.

This doesn't mean "expensive" or even "top of the line". Just don't buy the cheapest item out there and expect it to work just as well as a higher-quality item. Things like speakers, microphones and mixers are complicated pieces of electrical equipment that can break down and die at the worst possible times.

Shop around and see what's available in your price range. Often music stores will let you take stuff home for a weekend and try it out. They will also let you "trade up" after you have bought and used a starter set.

Let's go over the basics in more detail and see what's required to get the music started.

Speakers

The first time I walked into a music store in search of speakers I was intimidated. I knew I wanted "big, powerful" speakers, but I had no idea how big or how powerful. The most important thing to look for when you are shopping for speakers is the wattage. Generally, the more the watts, the louder it will be. Remember, your speakers should be to be loud but clear. The only thing worse than bad music is bad loud music. We usually use two 150-watt speakers and a 100-watt mixer for most gigs. (The mixer is described below in the next section). You just add the watts together for the total power. A 100-watt mixer plus two 150-watt speakers equals 400 watts total power.

400 watts is sufficient power to work a gig in a community hall where you have about 100-200 people. In a regular-sized community hall, the 2 speakers and the mixer would run at 50-70 per cent of capacity – that is, we could go even louder if we wanted to. If you run right at the maximum volume, you run the risk of either burning out your equipment or having it "hiss" or sound rough.

You also should be aware that if you have a huge sound system but are playing a tiny venue (such as a small pub or pool party), turning down your system to 10 per cent of capacity can also cause sound quality problems such as hissing or sounding tinny. It would be like buying a high-end sports car and then revving it in the garage—that thing is designed for the highway! The best way to figure out what works is to test your system at home or at an empty community hall, warehouse, or even a well-insulated garage and write down the settings that you like. You can have different settings written down in advance, and then when you do a gig it is just a matter of tweaking them slightly to see what sounds good at the venue. I always have a starting point default setting that I use for regular community halls—it is a setting that I know will sound great from about 30 yards away, but it leaves me lots of room to change, depending on the number of people in the room. You can also tweak the settings during the gig. It is always a good idea to walk around during an event and see how it sounds from different parts of the room (even if you have done this during a sound check).

If you wanted to work a really large party (over two hundred people), consider buying two more 150-watt speakers. This would mean that you would have four 150-watt speakers (an extra 300 watts to add to the equation), giving you 700 watts total when you add in a 100-watt mixer. That should blow the roof of a smaller community hall and would work just fine for a larger gig.

Mixers

If you have a weekend to kill, walk into a music store and ask them to show you some different mixers. You can spend hours in music stores seeing all of the different options available for deejays, musicians and sound board engineers.

What exactly is a mixer? Simply put, a mixer is the "in-between" part that links your computer (an input) and microphone (another input) to your speakers (the output). Without it, you would need a set of speakers to hear someone speak from the microphone, and another set to hear the music coming from your computer (or other output device). A basic 4-channel mixer is a box that provides amplified power to the speakers. You can pretty much hook up anything to a mixer – a computer, microphone, keyboard, guitars—the list is endless. If you have ever seen a documentary about recording an album, you have probably seen a stressed out music producer huddled over a 24-channel mixer. These huge machines can synchronize 24 different inputs—while the band wails away on a guitar, beats the drums and tickles the ivories, the sound engineer is running all of these different sounds into the mixer, where he can adjust the treble, bass, volume and reverb.

For the basic DJ, all you need is a simple 4-channel mixer. You can buy a 4-channel mixer and two good quality speakers as a package from a music store for under $1,000. Some people might try to sell you used mixers or speakers. Buyer beware! Spend the extra few hundred dollars and get good quality speakers and a good mixer. That way, you can look after them and you know that they will work for a long time. There are a lot of things that you cannot control at a function, but generally speaking, you can control how well you look after gear over the long run.

If you are not sure what constitutes a "good" quality speaker, shop around. Invest the time early on to learning about speakers. Go into a music store and see what shops are selling. Ask the sales guys. Chances are good that the cheaper stuff is inexpensive for a reason. I'm not suggesting that you blow the bank on the best-quality items out there, but there's no point in saving a couple of hundred dollars on a small set of speakers and a mixer that will only bring you frustration because it doesn't sound good at an average-sized venue. .

Ask the music store if you can try out the speakers and the mixer at home for the weekend. You may have to give them a deposit, but it's worth it to find out if you really want to invest a thousand dollars in your most important pieces of equipment.

Microphones

I learned the hard way to buy a good microphone. I was DJing a wedding and one of the guests wanted to sing a song for the bride and groom. This nice guy came up on stage with their acoustic guitar and their sheet music, ready to impress the group of about two hundred and fifty people. He was quite nervous and I tweaked the settings on the mixer for the microphone, waiting for their voice to fill the community hall.

Well, I was handed a nasty surprise. The cheap starter microphone that I bought at the local Radio Shack for $20 started cutting out. He sang his two-minute song, but to me it felt like an eternity. Of course, I didn't have a backup. Who brings a backup microphone, I wondered? Hopefully you will.

A friend of mine who runs a local band gave me an old microphone that he had on hand after I told him about the fiasco the day after the gig. He told me that one of the most common problems that bands have are technical difficulties with cheap equipment, and microphones are right at the top of the list. His old, beat up microphone was purchased at a high-end music store and it has worked great ever since. This mike is practically indestructible—it's the type that professional bands use, and people can twirl it, throw it around or bump it, and it just keeps on working.

Spend the money and time to do it right the first time. Tell the guy at the music store that you are in a rock band and that you will be spinning the microphone around and it might even get knocked about. You want to have a microphone that will survive any bumps and bruises that will happen. Look the other way when you see the $20 discount starter mike at the local shop.

Microphone Stand

This is an absolute necessity. People at weddings and parties will want to get up on stage to talk to their guests, and you may be called upon to give out door prizes, do some draws or even "warm up" the crowd under certain circumstances. A microphone stand will keep people's hands off of the microphone. What I mean by that is that people will not physically touch the microphone—they may talk into it, but they won't be dropping it or otherwise moving it around without necessity. The last thing you want is someone holding your mike and then dropping it on stage. If they are reading from a piece of paper, which happens at just about every wedding, they can hold the paper and let the microphone stand do its job.

You can buy a good, metal microphone stand at any music store or Radio Shack. They usually cost about $50. Sometimes the stand comes with the microphone clip on the top to hold the actual microphone, and sometimes it doesn't. Make sure to check. The clip is usually black and screws into the top of the microphone stand. It runs about $10.

Computer

I've heard people recently say that with the huge popularity of digital music such as the iPod and mp3 players, that you don't need a computer in order to DJ. While that may be true someday, I would still suggest getting a good quality computer. The reason for this is that with a computer, you can still play CDs. It is a virtual guarantee that at some point, you will get a gig where the client asks you to play music that you have never heard of before. It may be obscure maritime jigs, African tribal dance fusion or even a local artist who has their own CD. (This happens quite a bit—I am always amazed by local people who are accountants or carpenters and they have a little CD with their own songs—and often they sound great!) In these cases, you can simply take the client's CD and just download into your computer, sometimes even on the night of the gig. (Although I prefer to do this weeks in advance, which gives you time to listen to the songs. I hate surprises at DJ gigs, like tracks skipping, sudden profanity on a song or not knowing if the song is a ballad or a fast dance track.)

A good quality computer does not have to be expensive. For a first couple of years that I was DJing, I used a big, clunky desktop computer. It had a huge 30-pound monitor that could barely fit into the back seat of a car. No one cared except me, who was out of breath every time I had a gig because lugging the computer monitor into various community halls was a lot of work. I finally bought a laptop and the setup time was cut in half.

I can guarantee you that technology will advance, and in five years from now there will be another crazy invention that will allow some teenager to have even more songs in a one-ounce device that he holds in the palm of his hand. However, there might not be any DJ software on the mp3 players. This is the other reason that I enjoy using a computer for DJing—you can use DJ software to mix songs. This is similar to what the radios do. Have you noticed that often a song will fade out and then, before the song is completely gone, the other track starts up? This is the concept of "continuous music" and it is big with DJs. If you want to completely kill the momentum of a party, let a great dance track fade out for twenty seconds. You can actually see the life in the party fade away. With DJ software, you can let the dance track fade out, but as soon as it gets a little quiet you can fade in another great dance track!

People will keep dancing all night as you quickly replace one great track with the next. Dead air is called "dead" for a reason.

DJ software is not expensive. In fact, you can get DJ software on the internet for free. I have used a program called *KraMixer* and *MixVibes* and they were both free. See the appendix at the end of this book for more references to DJ tools and software that will help you get started.

Make sure that your computer has a CD-ROM drive on it—this allows you to dump music into your computer and / or play CDs. There are seemingly endless varieties of software out there that will help you catalogue songs and burn music. I've never paid for any of the software. There are programs on the internet called "freeware" and they are perfectly legal computer applications that are written by people who want to share their ideas with the world. Sometimes the authors of the software ask for a voluntary donation if you like their programs. They post their programs online on their websites and are available for download. Again, this will be discussed in the section "DJ software" later in the book.

Power Cords, Cables & Music Supplies

These are the little things that no one really thinks about until you need them. These are things like power cords, batteries and extension cords. Buy a couple of really good extension cords that are long (like thirty feet or so). One of the most stressful experiences you can have is getting to a community hall or venue and finding out that the plug-ins are nowhere to be found, or worse, people are walking over them all night. Buy some duct tape, packing tape or fat masking tape to make sure that the cords stay locked in position for the evening. You don't need people accidentally kicking out a plug.

A pen and paper are also essential. For my gigs, which were almost always a two-person job, we would write down the songs that we played in the order that we played them. We would also rate them and then note which songs really got the crowd pumped up and which ones were duds. This way, we could focus our attention to other things (like customer service and having a good time) and not trying to remember every little thing that happened during the night, since it was written down.

A pen and paper is also useful to write down notes at the last minute, such as the names of the people you are dealing with. You will know the basics about your client and their family or situation (hopefully) but maybe you will need to talk with the manager at the hotel or even jot down the name of the busboy or server. You never know when you may need to lean on them for an extra chair, table or lamp if you hit a snag somewhere along the way.

We also brought along a small electric fan to some of the community halls that we know are warm in the summer (and sometimes even in the winter). This makes a big difference if you are sweaty and nervous!

Other small items include a change of clothes, a water bottle, Aspirin or similar pain medication, a small lamp, and some cash in your wallet. Chances are that you may not need any of these things, but by packing a small box with these items, you avoid a disaster.

A Vehicle

You must have reliable transportation if you want to be a DJ. You are not walking on a bus with a computer and speakers. Reliable transportation means having a vehicle that can transport you, your partner (if the gig is a two-person job) and all of your gear safely. Make sure that you have a backup plan in case your vehicle won't work or someone else is using it. This may mean renting a vehicle for the weekend or even calling a taxi. Do this research ahead of time so that you aren't scrambling at the last minute to get to your gig.

Business Cards

This is a really inexpensive way to promote your business. Go to a business store and get 1,000 cards printed—it will probably cost about $20 to $30. If you are savvy with a computer, you can even print them yourself.

Make sure that they are professional and include your name, phone number and email address (or any other way that people can get a hold of you, such as a website). There are no hard and fast rules, so feel free to print wild and colorful cards if that is your personality—as long as they are easy to read and have your correct information on there. Let me repeat: all of the critical information must be on your card. The potential client must be able to easily get a hold of you should they want to book your gig.

Catalogue

A big part of being a DJ means taking requests. If you think that you are just going to spend the night playing all of the songs that you like, think again. If that was the case, the client would just plug in a CD player into the wall and hit "random" with their favorite CDs or mp3 files in there. Anyone with a power cord can hook up their iPhone to a house speaker system and blast Top 40 tracks to fill a room. Clients are paying you money to provide a specific service, and as such it is usually expected that you will be playing requests.

An easy way to show your customers which songs you have is to put your songs into a spreadsheet (such as Excel) and then sort them alphabetically. Admittedly, this is quite a bit of work. To catalogue 1,000 artists and song names will probably take you all day if not the whole weekend. If you are more tech-savvy and can download your tracks into another form on the computer, then go for it. The important thing is to have something in hard copy (paper) that the client can leaf through. Showing them a computer screen of your songs will not work—most people will stand there and flip through your catalogue, or even take it back to their table where people can eyeball it over a couple of drinks. Bring a couple of catalogues in case one gets "borrowed" or a drink gets spilled on it. If your catalogue gets damaged at a gig, throw it up and re-print another one.

I catalogued our songs into different categories such as classic rock, modern, dance and country. I would also recommend creating a "top 10" or "top 20" chart of the best of each category. This way, if a customer is in a hurry or doesn't want to look through the whole 20 or 30-page catalogue, they can browse the "top 10" list and pick from that. Most people are either in a hurry, drunk, or impatient (or all three) and looking at a "best of" list is easy and quick.

Additional Things

In addition to the basics, there some "extras" that you could consider purchasing / renting / using if you like. They are:

Display sign:"Who was that masked DJ?" There's nothing worse than having a great gig, blowing the crowd away with your rocking tunes, and then not getting any follow up business because no one at the party knew who you were. Make sure to purchase a sign that clearly shows the name of your business, and/or the website of your company.

Lights: This is an "extra" because most DJs starting out don't need this. However, if you can purchase a couple of colorful lights and have the space to transport them, they can provide value for the customer and really add to the experience. Most lights are stand-alone units that twirl colors or flash intermittently.

Smoke machine: This is definitely an "extra"—most startups do not worry about such extravagancies. However, a smoke machine can be a really cool extra for certain parties like Halloween or school dances.

Disco ball: A disco ball works well in conjunction with a strobe or powerful light. When the light hits the mirrored ball, the entire room lights up with tiny blobs of light. The effect can be dramatic. Make sure that if you are using the disco ball that you have a ladder that is capable of reaching the top of the dance hall or community hall that you are playing.

Promotional items: These would include putting your company decal on the side of your vehicle, giving out promotional stickers or fridge magnets, or creating a website. The idea here is to clearly display your company name, that fact that you provide DJ services, and your contact info such as a phone number or a website. There are lots of promotional items like pamphlets, coupons, matchbooks, pencils, pens, stickers, magnets—and many of them are quite inexpensive to get printed.

Party favors / door prizes: Try purchasing some wrapped candy and putting a few pieces in colorful sacks or baggies, and then tying them up with ribbon with your business card attached. Chances are good that kids will see them on the tables at the dances and will untie the bag. As they eat the candy, people will notice the business card. There are many similar ideas that you can use. Be creative—is there a trinket that you can make or buy for a little money that you can attach a business card to? Maybe you can get your logo printed on coffee mugs and give them away as prizes at the dances (if it is OK with the client; usually they are happy for extra prizes). Pens, pencils, felt-tip markers, T-shirts, magnets... the list of promotional items that you can inscribe with your logo is endless.

High-End Versus Low-End

"High-end" services mean basically that you, as the business, are providing a wide range of services that commands an expensive fee. "Low-end", on the other hand, means that you are providing basic services for a less expensive fee.

An analogy can be used from the restaurant industry. Some people really enjoy going out to a fancy restaurant and spending $250 for dinner for two. They like to dress up, enjoy four courses of incredible food, have a great atmosphere—they like the regal feeling that comes with spending a lot of money at a fancy restaurant.

Other people like to eat a great quantity of food and not spend much money while doing it. To them, quality is not as important as quantity. Have you ever seen a family of five at the "all-you-can-eat" buffet? While the place is clean and the food is good, they are probably more

Karl Wiebe

budget-conscious than quality-conscious. They want to get fed quickly and cheaply.

Neither one of these scenarios is better than the other one from a business perspective. They are both appealing—provided that the demand is there for either one of them. McDonald's, Burger King and Wendy's have become hugely successful restaurant chains because they offer popular food at very reasonable prices. On the other hand, there are privately owned, very expensive restaurants in your local city that are also very profitable. Granted, they probably cost much more to run, since they need to hire a world-class chef, a well-paid staff to keep the restaurant immaculate, and they need to purchase fancy soaps for the bathrooms. But they also charge way, way more for a meal than the burger restaurants. As long as both restaurants make money and pull a profit, they are good business models.

The same is true in the DJ world. There are DJ businesses that offer the "bare bones" services—that is, they play lots of music and provide a microphone stand for a set number of hours. They charge a fee, and that fee is almost always among the lowest in the city. There are other DJs who charge more—sometimes substantially more—and offer more in return, such as lights, a smoke machine and some party favors such a dancers, a video screen, games, and prizes. Still others provide services that aren't just associated with DJing, such as wedding or party photography services, emceeing / hosting an event (introducing certain guests, asking people to be seated, and keeping the evening "moving along"), food and beverage service, and full-on party planning and event coordinating.

When deciding what type of business model to run, consider your experience in the industry, your related skills, and the time and energy

34

you are willing and able to put in to such a venture. When in doubt, start small. Charge less money and you are virtually guaranteed to get a gig here and there to start—there are always people out there who just want a "bare bones" DJ to come spin some tunes at a party. I've found this to be especially true at community halls, where they are operating on a fixed budget or have very little money to spend. Most of the time, these venues just want a cheap DJ to show up on time. Once you get some experience, buy more equipment, invest in some other services, or otherwise expand your business, than you can charge more money and grow your business revenues accordingly.

Remember, the marketing and research for a DJ business is the most important part of the whole process—and it takes place at the start, before you buy a bunch of gear and invest money in a website, an automobile and 3,000 fridge magnets. Marketing is the process of researching the customer. Who are they? Who are these people who are willing to spend money to have you show up and press play? What sorts of services and products will they buy and why? Without proper marketing, you are basically spending a few thousand dollars on CDs, hardware, software, a computer, speakers and all the business supplies and then hoping that people will line up and pay you money to DJ. It is just not that easy. However, if you research your city or town and determine that there is a demand for your services, then you are ready to get serious about making the investment of time, money and energy into this potentially very rewarding industry.

Chapter 2:
Getting The Gigs

There are all sorts of events that require a DJ. The important thing to remember is that the event in question must be something that you feel comfortable doing, and that you feel you can provide a good product or service for the customer.

This might mean that there will be some gigs that you turn down. This was a hard lesson for me to learn. I found that when I first started out, I wanted to earn as much money as possible since I had paid a substantial amount of money for my DJ equipment. However, I took an inventory of what I was comfortable doing, and realized that I did not want to perform certain events such as high maintenance weddings or school dances. I turned down my first gig after a stressful conversation with a wedding planner one evening. She wanted to hire our DJ services for a wedding, but the bride and groom wanted very specific songs played, and in a certain order.

My warning flags went up. If the client wanted a jukebox, why not just rent your own DJ equipment, load up the songs and press play? People hire DJs to take requests and play music that will stimulate a party. I didn't want to sit in a hall and watch a digital play list unfold throughout the night. Besides, what could I say if a guest at the wedding reception wanted to make a request? "Sorry, but I've pre-programmed a bunch of songs for the bride and groom and they've asked me to play them in a very specific order"? It didn't sound like much fun, and I also figured that even if I performed the job adequately, many people might perceive the DJ as being inflexible and not very entertaining. It could hurt future business for me. I didn't want partygoers to think that the services that we were providing were rigid and boring.

I declined the offer of DJing the wedding. In this case, it was relatively easy to do since the songs that they were requesting were obscure anyway. My opinion was that the entire night was an entertainment disaster waiting to happen, and I was glad that I didn't take the gig. Life is too short for that kind of stress.

What sort of events do you feel most comfortable DJing? Are you a country-music specialist? If you enjoy current music, maybe school dances would be more to your liking than other events that cater to an older generation. Some DJs do not have a preference and enjoy all sorts of music, although these DJs (just like people in general) are somewhat rare.

Get It In Writing: The DJ Contract

Most people in life hate confrontation. They will just agree with someone because they don't want to hurt someone's feelings, or they don't want a fight on their hands. Also, most people "want to believe". They want to believe that clients are well-meaning and trustworthy, and that they will be just as professional and you will be.

Don't you believe it. They are looking out for themselves when they are planning an event and want the most services for the least amount of money. Can you blame them?

For every event that you perform, you should have a written contract. I've heard of many DJs and bands who have agreed to do a gig for a "buddy" only to find that the whole event fell through about a week before the event was scheduled. "Sorry, we don't need you anymore!" your friend the promoter says, and you are out of a night's work. And since the cancelled date was only a few days away, there is no way you are going to fill it. Instead of earning great money, you are spending Saturday night watching television.

Get the contract signed and include a non-refundable deposit. We would typically ask for $100 to hold the night. This way, if the client cancelled, we kept the $100. This is valuable around your busy times of year, such as the entire month of December, when hopefully you will be doing Christmas and holiday parties every weekend. The $100 is your "are you serious" money. If your client is not willing to put down $100, are they serous about their party or not? You are worth it.

There is a sample of a typical DJ contract on the following page. Make sure that the client signs a copy and sends it to you with a non-refundable deposit. This is the only way that you can protect yourself from last-minute cancellations that will leave you high and dry. You are not investing thousands of dollars and spending endless hours cataloging songs and learning the craft of DJing just to grab a quick $100. If the client does not trust you, and don't want to pay you the $100, then don't take the gig. That is a warning flag. You do not need the stress. I personally have never had a problem with people paying a small deposit—in fact, it is expected that a professional business will want a small deposit as a sign of good faith to "hold the date".

When you actually DJ the event, bring the contract along and keep it handy in case there is a discrepancy. On more than one occasion the client has forgotten how much the fee was, and I pulled out the contract from my back pocket and showed them. In many cases, like at weddings or community hall parties, the client is going through the bar till and peeling off hundreds and fifties to pay the DJ—it can be a little chaotic with the music going and the lights down. The last thing the event organizer is thinking about at 1 a.m. is how much your fee was. Bring the contract!

The contract also has your playing time written in there, so that if the event runs long, the client can ask you to play longer, but at least it is your choice and you have the right to ask for more money if you choose to do so.

SAMPLE CONTRACT / AGREEMENT

Date of agreement: July 10, 2012

Between ABC DJ SERVICE and SIGNAL HILL COMMUNITY CENTRE

IT IS MUTUALLY AGREED between the parties that:

- ABC DJ SERVICE will furnish, and the purchaser will accept, for the engagement hereinafter described, the services of ABC DJ SERVICE - Basic Deejay service (essentially 2 amplified speakers, one microphone, 2 deejays and a digital sound system containing more than 1,000 songs, and a catalogue of songs for requests).
- PURCHASER will supply table and 2 chairs for deejays, as well as reasonable access to plug-ins.
- Type of Function / Event: Community BBQ / Dance – July 15, 2005
- Address: SIGNAL HILL COMMUNITY CENTRE – 123 Any Lane
- Hours of Engagement: Total of 6 hours (approx 7 p.m. to approx 1 a.m.)
- Agreed Price: $350 (plus applicable taxes)
- Agreed Deposit to secure event: $100 (to be mailed or dropped off to address below)

PURCHASER WILL MAKE PAYMENT AS FOLLOWS:

CASH or CHECK made payable to "ABC DJ Service" or "John Smith"

upon completion of engagement ON THE NIGHT OF THE EVENT.

ABC DJ SERVICE at all times have complete supervision, direction and control over the services of its personnel on this engagement and expressly reserves the right to control the manner, means and details of the performance of services, as well as the ends to be accomplished. This includes the right to refuse to play certain songs for any reason (such as profanity or inappropriateness to the situation).

IT IS UNDERSTOOD that ABC DJ SERVICE (John Smith) executes this agreement as an independent contractor and is not an employee of the purchaser.

THE PURCHASER or ABC DJ SERVICE may cancel the engagement with 30 days written notice due to any unforeseen circumstances. Please note that $100 deposit is non-refundable in the case of cancellation by the client. In the case of cancellation by ABC DJ Service, the $100 is fully refundable as is interest on the deposit (prime business rate as determined by the Bank of Canada).

A sample contract for a DJ; make sure to get it in writing.

Although this may not happen to you, we actually had the DJ contract on hand to prove to the hotel manager that we were supposed to play until a set time at a really quiet Christmas party. The oil & gas company that we were DJing for had laid off some employees only a few weeks earlier (right before the holidays no less) and the mood at the holiday party was really sour. We started playing at 8:00 p.m. in a beautiful dance hall, surrounded by holly and Christmas lights, and by 10:30 p.m. pretty much everyone in the ballroom had slurped down their two free drinks and left. It was depressing. What started out as a party with 200 people had dwindled down to one table. There were about 8 people in the entire dance hall, and the hotel manager came up to us at around 11 p.m. and told us to shut it down; the night was over. I replied that I had a contract from the client to play until midnight, and that's what I was going to do. Between you and me, if the hotel manager had cut our power and told us to leave, we would have done so, since the party was such a flop and no one seemed to be having a good time (everyone had left with the exception of a few bitter employees over in the corner at one table). However, the client was paying us to play until midnight and I wanted to fulfill the contract. Besides, we used the time to try some new songs and gain some experience of how they sounded in a big room with big sound. We enjoyed just playing some music that we wanted to hear. It was fun and we made the best of it! I did not want to give the client any reason to ask for a partial refund—in fact, I wanted those bitter employees to go back to work and say, "well, at least the DJ finished out the night, he didn't take off!"

There are many different events that range from very structured and formal ceremonies to relatively easy going, informal get-togethers. The following describes what you can expect at different types of events, and the challenges and characteristics of each.

Wedding Receptions

Weddings are the big-money events, but they are also high-maintenance and filled with pressure. Tensions are usually quite high amongst people who are in the wedding party, and sometimes they will take out their stress on the catering, event staff and, yes, DJs. Remember, the clients are only supposed to have one shot at their perfect wedding day, and if you screw it up, everyone will remember it for the rest of their lives. Of course, this isn't actually true, but sometimes the people who are paying you are honestly thinking that. For the most part, however, you can alleviate much of this stress by some preparation and research. Ask your wedding party what songs they most want to hear and then play them early. Show up on time and be ready to play. This often means that you will show up, well-dressed and ready to go, only to sit around and wait for a while. You can't just sit there and look bored and read a book. Sometimes it is better if you are a two-person team; at least you have someone to talk with, or one of you can man the station while the other one walks around. Keep in mind that if you do these simple things (asking the client about their preferences and being on time), chances are good that the wedding party (the bride, groom and the best man and bridesmaid, as well as the parents) will see that you have the situation under control and will be ready to party instead of eyeballing you. Or, at the very least, they will leave you alone and go bug the catering people instead.

While there is no such thing as a typical wedding, there are some things that tend to happen quite frequently at wedding receptions. Early on, one of the first things I noticed is that wedding receptions almost always run late. If you sign a contract to play music from 9 pm to 2 am, for example, show up at 8:45 pm, be ready to go, and don't worry if you sit around for an hour while the bride and groom get their picture taken, the meal runs late, and the speeches run long. You are getting paid regardless, and your evening will end at 2 am whether you play a little music or a lot of music. Using the 9-p.m.-to-2-a.m. example, I would typically open up a "classical" or "background" play list and then just let that run quietly in the background while people are eating, cutting cake or doing whatever. No matter what happens, just smile and roll with it. Remember, you can't control the meal running late, or the limo showing up late, or uncle Johnny's speech from running late. (You do, however, have some say in the evening if you are the emcee—if you control the microphone and keep the festivities moving along, you can keep the evening from becoming painfully boring for most of the guests.)

For a wedding reception, there is some structure, even though every one of them is unique. The evening typically follows a pattern such as:

- Background music / dinner
- Speeches from friends & family
- First dance (bride & groom)
- Second dance (bridal party)
- Third dance (wedding party including parents)
- The general dance begins (everyone else)

For background music, I've found that any soft classical music, as well as popular modern music such as Enya and John Tesh work great. Any soft, romantic music will work. This would include "muzac", which are popular songs such as the Beatles and Elton John that have been redone without the lyrics. (This is the sort of music people often hear in elevators.) This is the music that people will pay very little attention to, as they are eating and visiting. The music should be soft and quiet. All you are doing is filling the background with noise before the bride and groom dance. Remember, you are not the show! Just be in the background.

The speeches at wedding receptions are typically run through the "house system" that is provided by the golf club, community hall or hotel ballroom. These buildings usually have top-rate speaking podiums and microphones that run through the house system and out through a sophisticated surround-sound system, or at least some professional-level speakers. These usually work great. If at all possible, encourage your clients to use these facilities as they should be included in the client's price of the rental of the hall. This way, when the family gives their speeches, you can shut down and take a break for a half hour or however long this part of the night lasts. Besides, it is very rare that you are going to have professional-level DJ equipment that rivals a huge clubhouse or professional rotary house. Let the house system run!

If the wedding party is running late, and you are not the emcee, it's no big deal. It's not your wedding. This almost always happens—some uncle or long-lost relative has had a couple of beers and suddenly remembered a hilarious anecdote that takes way too long to tell. Use this time wisely to double-check your system settings or just relax.

Sometimes the client will offer you a meal or free drinks throughout the night. If they offer you food, fell free to take them up on it. The meals at wedding receptions are usually terrific, and you need to keep your strength up as the night will usually be five or six hours long. Make sure to drink a lot as well—but it should be water, juice or soft drinks. If you do have alcohol, make sure it's just one or two drinks at most throughout the night. Even if you could physically handle more, you want to maintain a professional atmosphere and you don't want to look like you are taking advantage of the client's generosity. There are always one or two bored relative sitting around, seemingly waiting to see if one of the people at the event does something a little weird. Don't give them any ammunition.

After the speeches, it is usually time for the first dance. This song should be picked out by the client (specifically the bride and groom) in advance. If there is an MC for the wedding, indicate to them that the first dance is going to start and they can introduce it, or you can if you like (check with the emcee as they may want to introduce everything—there could be a story or joke or some entertainment to go along with the song).

Usually the second dance is for the wedding party, which means that the bride and groom will dance, but they will be joined by the bridesmaid and best man, as well as anyone else who is in the wedding party. This song as well should be picked out by the client and virtually always is. In the extremely rare event that they don't know what song to use, see the appendix for suitable songs or just pick a sentimental (but not too romantic) song.

The third dance is similar to the second one, but this one has the addition of the bride and groom's parents. Again, this song should be chosen by the client and should be more sentimental than romantic.

After the first three songs, you can typically kick it up into high gear right away with three dance songs that are older in nature. 1970s rock, disco classics or some "sing-along" songs are great ("well... you know you make me wanna SHOUT!"). People at the wedding have been sitting and are excited and want to share in the fun. Ratchet up the speed and energy of the dance.

After three fast party songs, sprinkle in a ballad here and there. You will typically get two types of dancers: someone who will dance all night long to fast songs, and the reluctant husband who will only get up for a ballad in order to make his wife happy. You should strive to maintain a variety of songs throughout the first half of the evening, but make sure to play lots of songs early in the night for the senior citizens. This would mean songs like 1950s or 1960s classics—the Beatles, Beach Boys, and Isley Brothers are usually big hits at weddings. Play the most popular of these songs.

The seniors will usually call it a night by 11 pm. When this happens (you will see a steady stream of older people hugging and kissing the bride and heading for the door) then feel free to bring in some heavier dance songs and some more modern stuff.

Make sure to include classic wedding favorites such as the Bird Dance, Twist & Shout and Boney M's Rasputin. You will find that certain songs are "home runs"—that is, they virtually always get people up on the dance floor. Make sure to "hit a home run" every few songs so that the party continues to rock.

Check out the appendix at the end of this book to see a typical "wedding checklist" from the point of view of the consumer. It usually helps if you can look at the event from the eyes of a customer.

Birthday Parties

These type of events are varied because it completely depends on how old the person of honor is turning. A birthday party for a 90-year-old grandma is completely different than little Jenny's 10th birthday party. However, even these widely varying events have some common denominators that you can use as a guide.

The first thing to note with a birthday party is that you should play a bunch of songs that the client has requested. If it is a birthday party for an older person (like Grandma) and there is a wide range of ages attending, then of course you would play a mix, but you should know in advance that Grandma's favorite artists are Rod Stewart and the Beach Boys, for example. This way, any time there's a special moment (like cake, or presents, etc) you can play a signature song that everyone will know "is just for her".

Awards Ceremonies

These events are usually characterized by much waiting, since a significant portion of the gig is spent watching people get awards. This might be the case at a service awards function for a company, or a sports team who is having a dinner / dance at the end of their season. In these cases, the first half of the night is usually spent eating dinner and listening to speeches. If this is the case, you are relegated to backup music or dinner music (if any) until the awards are basically over. You might play the occasional "acceptance award" music, or maybe a short piece of music if the featured speaker is arriving to the podium. Then, if a dance or mingling follows, then you would play music accordingly. Note that music for mingling is much different than that of a dance. Light rock or mellow pop tunes should accent such an evening, but stay away from disco or heavier dance tunes if a dance is not in order.

Sporting Events

A sporting event such as a tailgate party before a big game can be really fun, as everyone who is there is in the mood to party (hopefully).

The goal here is just to provide some rocking background music before the game starts, so you would probably play some heavy rock music, current pop hits or even some old classic rock songs that are "sing-along" in nature. The important thing to remember here is that no one will dance; people are at the tailgate party to get ready for the big game and you are providing some fun background noise. Don't be surprised if no one even pays any attention to you. These can be really low-pressure events because you can basically be a radio in the background and just rock out.

Barbeques / Outdoor Festivals

These events are similar to the tailgate parties, although the music can be radically different, depending on the type of event and who is attending. Most people at a festival won't be there specifically to see you or hear your music, so you will probably be playing background / atmosphere music. There won't be much dancing. Usually soft rock or pop is the order of the day at this sort of event.

Halloween / Christmas Parties

These are more structured events that are put on by a dance hall, community organization, school or place of work. There are usually door prizes and speeches. There are some Halloween-oriented songs that should be played at such dances, and they are found in Chapter 6 ("The Music"). The same applies for Christmas parties. It is interesting to note that at some workplace parties, it will be known as "holiday" parties, with no mention of Christmas or any other religion. As such, there are "holiday-oriented" songs that you can play (again, see Chapter 6 "The Music") that will help make the party fun.

The Club DJ: Getting Experience

Have you ever wanted to DJ in a nightclub or a bar? Most of us picture a cigar-chomping nightclub owner telling us to get lost until we get some more experience. But how are we supposed to get experience as a club DJ if we can't get any gigs?

One way is to practice, practice and practice some more. DJ for your friends. DJ and put mixes down on tape or CD. Ask for feedback. Learn and grow.

There are jobs out there in the music industry, but they are in the background. Many people get their start by working in a bar or nightclub and watching the DJ work the room. Bars and nightclubs need audio-visual people to work the lights, and many mobile DJ services are looking to hire new workers. While the pay is low, you have to factor in the experience and education as well. It's like getting paid to go to school.

There are many jobs in the industry that have nothing to do with music, but still get you inside the bar. Dishwashers, bartenders, bouncers... usually the industry is in need of good workers because the low wages, long hours and high turnover.

Of course, you don't need to work to hang out in a nightclub. You can just go to the local bar on a Friday or Saturday night, grab a chair near the DJ and take notes. What works? What didn't? And why?

The internet is a great place for feedback, blogging and discussing tips and tricks. There are many different chat rooms and newsgroups that you can join and ask questions, offer your opinion, and share stories and tips. Just google "DJ opinion forum" and spend the next three days surfing through endless blogs, opinion pages and posts.

The most important thing is to develop an ear for what rocks and what doesn't, and to understand why. Not everyone will agree on what makes a great DJ, but if you study a few successful DJs in action, you should be able to hear what works and what doesn't. It might even be fun to watch a not-so-good DJ clear the dance floor, and learn from their mistakes.

Playing The Empty Room

I went to see a stand-up comic perform in town one night during the week. It was a Tuesday night at about 8:00 p.m. and there were literally ten people in the bar—maybe fifteen if you included the waiters and the bartender in the back. After the two opening acts, who were local up-and-coming comics, the headliner came out. He was from New York City and had worked on the hit show *Seinfeld*, had written for other television shows, and traveled North America doing stand up in all sorts of bars, nightclubs and comedy clubs. He was a big deal and I was excited to see him.

And here he was in front of ten people in a dark comedy club on a Tuesday night. I thought it was going to be uncomfortable. I felt at first like I was sitting in someone's basement listening to a friend try to do stand up. His set killed—he was well-spoken, intelligent, witty and absolutely hilarious. However, with only ten people in the room, it wasn't like he brought the house down.

I e-mailed him after his set and told him how much I liked his material. I said that it was too bad that there were only ten people in the whole bar that night, but I at least enjoyed the show. His response surprised me.

He said that he loved working during the week, because he fully expected no one to be there at his shows. Weeknights were an opportunity for him to try out new material and take chances that he normally could not do during the big shows on the weekends. With a packed house on Friday and Saturday nights, he pretty much had to stick to his proven material. If he was going to go down in flames with some new material, it would almost always be on a weeknight. That was where the truly great gems were found—during the times he could experiment a little bit and try new things out.

During your DJ career, you will undoubtedly come across a similar experience. Use an empty or almost-dead room to your advantage. Try some new material, new remixes, or different arrangements. What's the worst that is going to happen? If you know that the gig is going to be slow, bring along a new employee or a friend who wants to help and give them the reins at some point during the night. You just may find the next killer groove or three-song set that will knock everyone's socks off the next time you play a full house on the weekend.

Slow nights at the bar or at the hotel are also excellent opportunities to meet and work with the staff. If you get a recurring gig at a community hall, hotel ballroom or nightclub, make sure to familiarize yourself with the staff. Ask for feedback. You never know when you may need to call on a staff member to help you out of a jam.

If you are interested in the business-side of nightclubs or hotels, ask yourself (or even the manager) why it is a slow night. You can use the time to learn about the industry and the business.

Working a slow night and giving it your all will also showcase your talent to the owner or manager working the club. If you treat it with a passion and take a slow night seriously, chances are good that the owner or operator will know that you are ready to headline on the weekend, when the crowds are out in full force.

The Nightclub DJ

Playing a corporate gig can be a great night filled with radio-friendly music, at the end of which you collect a big paycheck. Or, it can be a boring, rigid gathering of old people who want to hear safe songs.

The truth is, most corporate gigs are both of these. If you are interested in playing clubs, it is a completely different crowd. People at a club are there to experience and enjoy different things from a corporate event.

The owner of the nightclub or bar will have a vision of what he wants the club to be, how it should appear, and what the bar's image will be. How is the club advertised? What are the themes inside the club? Most importantly, who frequents the club? What do the "regulars" like in terms of dance music, experience, and culture?

These are the variables that a DJ generally cannot control. The club DJ must adapt to the existing scene and create a name for themselves within the confines of the owner's image of the club.

Why is all of this so important? At the end of the gig, you probably want the owner to offer you a permanent or recurring gig. This is a steady paycheck and will mean that you can bank on some solid earnings in order to grow your business (and pay some bills).

You should be aware of the "non-regular" people that will enter a club but won't be coming back. They might not like the house music that you are providing and will try to badger you into trying to change it. If a nightclub is known for a certain style or sound, don't play requests that don't fit that style. Contrasting styles affects the image of the club and won't help business—it just might drive away confused customers.

If this sounds counter-intuitive, remember that DJing for a club is different than DJing at a corporate gig. At corporate events, such as weddings and community hall parties, you are being paid to take requests and make all of the guests happy (or at least as many people as possible). At clubs, however, you are being paid to broadcast the house style for the regular (and returning) patrons. Think of it in terms of a radio station— you probably have a favorite radio station, be it a country & western, rock, or pop station. How much would you like that station if they continually changed up the genre of music?

Not all nightclubs are created equal. Like many businesses, the ownership of any nightclub or bar sets the tone of the establishment. Some owners are old pros who purchase the bar (or a chain of bars) and as such have created a string of similar nightclubs. Others purchase multiple bars and then have different images for each one, with the hopes being that if a patron doesn't like one type of bar or pub, they will like another.

Working for an experienced club owner can have its advantages. If the nightclub is successful already, there will probably be an established base of customers that will make it easier to bring in customers and keep the club full. A full bar or nightclub also means that your chances of getting paid is much better, and chances are that the amount you get paid will be more than if you are working with a struggling or new nightclub. Working for a chain or group of bars can be a great way to get more paying gigs. If the bars are different in image, it will be up to you to show that you can play different styles to different crowds, if that is the direction that you want to take your business. Do you want to specialize in one area of club DJing? A generalist will get more paying gigs on average, but a specialist might be able to command more money on a per-gig basis, especially if they are able to make a name for themselves.

There are also some disadvantages to working for a successful club or bar. For example, the owner might have a set way of doing things, and that way might not be what you would consider the best way. However, their bar is successful, so they probably won't want to change the way they do things. It could be a "take it or leave it" job, meaning that if you don't take it, someone else will.

Often, successful nightclubs can pay less than a struggling nightclub. If this sounds strange, then welcome to the music industry. The rationale behind this would be that if you are playing a packed house, it is the bar and the location that is drawing in the crowds, and management doesn't really need you. Any old DJ will do, since they are already so popular! The same is true with an unsuccessful bar or a nightclub that is experiencing a slow night. Management will be reluctant to pay you top dollar when the night is slow, because they can't afford it, but will also be reluctant to pay you a big money when the place is full, since on Friday and Saturday nights the place is bulging at the seams anyway. The trick is finding a way to convince the ownership group that you are valuable; the when the house is packed, it is in part due to your musical skills.

The Nightclub Culture

Working nightclubs can either be some of the greatest gigs you do, or they can be a total nightmare. Bars have their own culture and you should try to familiarize yourself with that culture from the standpoint of an independent contractor, operator, or employee.

Don't be surprised or insulted if you are treated rudely or indifferently by security staff or wait staff. The industry is generally characterized by a "look out for number one" mentality. Some nightclub owners or employees might be crying out "that's not true!" but if that is the case, then consider yourself either very lucky or very, very lucky. It's not true in every case, but in at least some cases, nightclubs can be a rude and quirky environment.

Fights often break out at clubs. Make sure that if you bring your own gear, it is insured. Don't bother asking the ownership group or the nightclub manager to make sure that your gear is somehow protected. Chances are that if there is an expense to be paid, the manager will come up with some reason to not pay it. Are you going to sit in small claims court over a $300 speaker? I doubt it, especially if word gets out that you sued the owner. Most bar owners are notorious for being cheap and having a spotty memory at best—unless they are slighted, in which case they have a photographic memory! Just get your own gear insured up front, so that if a speaker gets bumped or a microphone is destroyed, stolen or mysteriously disappears, you can replace it.

Don't help the security guards if a fight breaks out. Don't be a hero. I repeat, do not be hero and jeopardize your health and safety. The only exception to this would be if it is somehow written into your job description. Security guards generally know what they are doing. If you see a fight, just call over security, alert them to the problem, and then get out of their way. You would not like it if someone "helped" you spin tunes, so respect the security guards and let them be professionals.

Like any business that serves alcohol, there are provincial and federal guidelines about what you can and cannot do at a nightclub. The most obvious one is the drinking age—serving alcohol to an underage person is against the law and there can be serious penalties if the nightclub is found to have done this. There are usually rules involving the hours of operation, employee conduct, when to cut off an intoxicated patron, indecency laws and acts of violence. It's always a good idea to familiarize yourself with the local laws so that you can protect yourself legally in the case of an incident. Remember, you can have fun, and might even be encouraged to have fun, but be professional first and foremost.

Waiters, waitresses, bartenders and even bouncers get tips in nightclubs. For many of them, it is a substantial amount of their employment income. If the club is busy, think about getting your own drink of water if you are able to leave your station. If a waiter or waitress gets you a drink, tip them.

Some customers may approach the club DJ and offer money to play different types of music. Sometimes the money is substantial. Check with the manager ahead of time about the strictness of music format. Don't change the music format and risk losing a future gig for a few bucks. Encourage the customer to either purchase more booze, or tip the wait staff. If the bar staff find out that you are on their side, you may be surprised by the amount of preferential treatment you can get (free drinks, a bouncer constantly walking by your DJ area to make sure you and your equipment is safe, et cetera).

Many night clubs and bars have a policy of cleaning up if you are working in a set DJ booth. If you are using their equipment, this one is a no-brainer. Leave the work environment spotless when you leave for the night. Turn off all amps and equipment, organize the shelves and desks, and return your empty glasses to the bar. If you are courteous, it will be noticed by staff. If you are not courteous, it will also be noticed by staff and probably the owner.

Some nightclubs employ spotters. These are people who pose as customers and basically walk around the bar, pretending to have a good time. They are actually working and will monitor wait staff, bouncers, bartenders, and even DJs. Make sure that you are courteous to all customers and be professional at all times—you never know who may be watching.

Chapter 3:
The Customer

A business literally starts with a customer. Without a sale, it is not really a business—it is just a hobby. Anyone can play music. If someone pays you money to play music, that is a business. Customers are the most important part of being a DJ, because without them, you are basically fooling around with a bunch of DJ equipment for free.

Are you a "people person"? For some of us, the answer is definitely yes. We enjoy talking to strangers, meeting new people, or dealing with clients.

For the rest of us, we don't really enjoy hanging out with strangers and for the most part would rather be by ourselves or with people that we know. It helps to know which type of person you are.

If you are not a "people person", don't worry. It's not like you can't be a DJ just because you don't light up in a room full of strangers. In fact, some could argue that "people persons" can be annoying because they want to be part of the party instead of work the party.

Remember this rule: *As a DJ, you are helping to make the party great, but you are working the party. Be professional.*

With that said, it should be mentioned that many high-end, successful band members and DJs have social skills that enable them to function in a group setting. While we may watch the television and laugh when punk bands give their audience the finger or swear at an awards show, you will, in all likelihood, not be working those types of events. Even if you are playing a hard-core, smoky, heavy-metal bar, in most cases the owner would want you to be able to communicate intelligently with the audience. Social skills are important.

One of the biggest mistakes that a new DJ can make is that they become part of the party. What might happen is that the customer will be having a huge barbeque or community hall party, and give you a dinner ticket in addition to your fee. There might also be a couple drink tickets handed out at the start of the night, or in some cases the client might even tell you to just help yourself to the bar, since you are part of the staff working and so you don't need to pay for drinks.

Don't take advantage of this situation. It may sound obvious, but I've heard many stories of DJs and band members getting completely bombed at these parties. It is like they have completely forgotten that they are there to do a job. If you can handle drinks, maybe limit yourself to one or two. I personally never drink on the job. I usually have a couple of pops or a juice and I will try to drink as much water as possible as it keeps me well-hydrated and lucid.

I would graciously accept a dinner invitation if the client offered it to us. Hey, a free meal is a free meal. But be reasonable—let the paying guests eat first and don't take more food at the buffet than you can eat. Always err on the side of being responsible, courteous and professional. You never know if there's a potential client standing behind you at the open bar or buffet table.

Troubleshooting: Dealing With Problem Scenarios

Even if you are not a "people person", to be successful in the DJ business, or any business for that matter, you will have to put customer service right at the top of your list. However, there are some situations that may arise that will present problems or challenges for you during the event. While this chapter won't cover them all, hopefully they can arm you somewhat for the inevitable hiccups that will occur during the events.

Problem: DJ Is Running Late

You will no doubt eventually show up late for an event. You might get there late because of bad traffic. Maybe your car broke down. Maybe there was a last-minute family emergency, or some other reason that you have no control over. However, you can minimize the severity of this problem by setting up your equipment for the gig in advance and checking everything before you leave. For example, if you set up in the afternoon for an evening gig, it probably means that you will have to make two trips to the function—once to set up in the afternoon and then again to actually DJ the event. This should be standard practice. When you DJ, hopefully you are wearing more formal clothes, such as a suit or business casual attire. If the event is more rocking in nature, like a heavy metal club or a bar, then dress appropriately. You definitely want to look professional but cool. (When you are doing set up and sound check a few hours earlier, you will probably be wearing jeans or some other casual wear.)

In my experience, typically, we would set up around 3 or 4 p.m. if the gig was at 9 p.m. This would mean that we would have about 4 or 5 hours in-between. I used this time to have a nap, eat a healthy meal and

The Digital DJ Handbook

relax before heading back to DJ. Making two trips also means that you will know exactly where the event is, since you have already been there once already to set up.

Problem: The Event Is Running Late

More likely than not, you will arrive on time and discover that the event itself is running late. The dinner that was supposed to start at 7 p.m. runs late, and as a result the dance party that was supposed to start at 9 p.m. isn't going to happen until 9:30 p.m. or even later. It has nothing to do with you, but everything is backed up.

Don't sweat it. You have your time written into your contract, and when your night is done, it is done. We would typically have a contracted time of 9 p.m. to 1 a.m., and then if the party ran late, we would play until 1:15 a.m. if everyone was having a great time. Often the customer would really appreciate this and it led to many word-of-mouth referrals. Us playing for an extra 15 minutes basically translated into extra revenue through more business. It was definitely time well spent, especially if the crowd and the client are appreciative. I can remember many nights where I would take the microphone, mention to the crowd that we were done, and thank them for a great evening. Then we would announce that as a thank you for being such a great crowd, we were playing three more songs as a thank you. People would cheer and we were heroes, but it also served as a "last call" to the patrons and event staff that the party was effectively ending.

It is important to note that in the beginning stages of any business, word-of-mouth referrals are the single most cost-effective way to increase your revenues. An extra fifteen minutes of playing could lead to a happy referral. Even if it doesn't, you will have given up very little and made the customer happy. A referral could come months or even years after a gig.

Problem: "Stump The DJ" Customer

One of the neat things about being a DJ is that you have a large arsenal of songs at your disposal. Unlike a band, who might know forty or fifty songs at most, a DJ can instantly play any one of hundreds and hundreds of songs. At almost every event, however, there is going to be someone who will ask you if you have "The Tomato Song" by some little known artist. You won't. Chances are that you have never heard of that song. It doesn't matter how many songs you have, they will request one that you don't have. You have never heard of it, and neither has anyone else.

In these instances, I've found that sometimes that person requesting the song genuinely would like to hear it and is surprised that you don't carry it. Other times, he or she is a bored party person who wants to be the one who can complain that "this DJ doesn't even play 'The Tomato Song!' What do you mean you have never heard of it?" Don't worry.

If the song is legitimate, tell them that you don't have it, but that you would be happy to play something else. If they are not happy with that, then there's not much that you can do. Offer them your catalogue, which should have hundreds of songs (some catalogues have literally over two thousand songs) and either they can pick something or they can go sit down. If I receive a request for a song that I have never heard of, I will write it down and research it either online to find out who sings it or what album it is from. If more than one person requests that song, we will usually make an effort to find it and add it to our collection. Your list of songs should always be growing anyway, so this is a natural part of the business. Don't get discouraged if you don't have a specific song; use it as a learning experience to make your business better in the future. Remember, if you have 1,000 songs or more at your disposal, the chances are good that they should be able to find one at least one that they like—unless they are completely miserable, in which case you cannot help them anyway.

A friend of mine who has played bass in a corporate party band for years told me that they get similar problems as well. He said that once, at a party, a woman came up to him and requested "anything by Michael Jackson". They didn't cover any Michael Jackson songs; they were mostly a country and classic rock band. Undeterred, she then asked for "anything by Madonna". Again, being a rock band, it wasn't going to happen, as both of these artists were considered "1980s / 1990s" retro-dance. The band played mostly rock songs. Disgusted, the lady walked away, exclaiming "you guys don't know anything!" This band had been playing gigs for twenty years and easily knew sixty to eighty songs. That is a pretty limited range if you are happy with only Michael Jackson or Madonna!

The point is, you are invariably going to run in to customers who want to hear something that you don't have. If you are honest, say that you don't have the song, and give them the catalogue, they will either find something else that they like, or leave. That is all you can do.

Problem: Chatty Or Lonely Customers

What happens if you are working at a party and someone is not having a good time? Maybe they are bored, had a bad day at work, or just got dumped by their girlfriend. Then, suddenly... they see you.

Often the DJ will attract the wallflowers, who buzz around the station and like to try to engage in conversation. After all, the DJ is just pressing a button and out comes the music, right? They don't see the hard work and preparation that goes into working a party. They might see you sitting there, not talking, and actually feel sorry for you! They will come over and strike up a conversation with you, and in their minds they are helping you out.

If you get a party person who is just loitering around your station, try to end the conversation if it is getting in the way of your job. You need to have one ear on the dance floor and another ear to deal with customers, and in most cases you won't have the time or energy to baby-sit a bored party person. Often older children will come up to the DJ booth and ask how every piece of equipment works. They are bored. Ask him or her if they are requesting a song. If they still don't get the message, thank them for the great conversation ("It was great talking with you, but...") and then explain that you have to get back to work. Be polite but firm. They are not paying you for your work, the client is.

Problem: Non-Stop Requests

One of the neat things about a DJ is that you can just shout a song at him through the fog, lights and loud music, and he will just play that song a few minutes later! It is just like a jukebox, and you don't even need to have a pocketful of quarters. Of course, we all know that DJing is not really like this, but people seem to forget once they have had a couple of drinks. If someone comes up and requests a song, and it fits in with your general idea of what the evening should be like, it goes without saying that you would want to play that song—eventually. However, you may find that the same person (or small group of people) just keep running back up to you and request song after song.

In this case, check them out to see if they are actually dancing. If they are just coming up from their table and requesting songs and then sitting back down, then chances are good that they are just bored and are not requesting songs to dance and enjoy the evening. Remember, if you are DJing a dance, your primary responsibility is to keep that dance floor rocking and full.

If you see that the same people are coming up again and again, the first step is to just stop playing their requests. You are running the show, not them. If they continue to ask when you are going to play their songs, mention to them that you already played their request (or multiple requests) earlier in the evening, and you are going to play other people's requests. (It doesn't matter if anyone else is actually coming up and requesting songs—you can just say that the client provided a list in advance.) In most cases, they will take the hint and leave you alone, realizing that they are not the only ones at the party.

There may be another variation on this theme if you are DJing a corporate Christmas party (or "holiday" parties as they are often now known). Sometimes the president of the company frequently visit you and offer "tips" to improve the music. This is understandable, since the president's job is to basically spend all day making decisions and telling other people what to do. Why should it be any different at the party? All you can do in this case is take their suggestion and do the best you can to accommodate them. After all, they are paying for the evening (if not personally, at least through their company). Try to be diplomatic and if it is getting in the way of people enjoying their evening, just tell the president that you have many requests and you are doing the best you can.

Problem: Children

Bright lights, loud music and a cool DJ! It is the perfect recipe for kids annoying you at a wedding or a party. Often the children's parents are nowhere to be seen, as they are having a good time and not thinking that their child is getting into trouble. Worse, some parents just don't care where their child is.

Having kids playing around your DJ equipment can be annoying, but they can also be dangerous. Electrical cables and delicate machinery should be considered "off limits" to all customers, kids or adults alike. I've seen children come up and start pressing buttons, messing with the microphone, and generally causing trouble, while their parents sit twenty yards away and watch, thinking that "little Johnny" is just adorable.

Don't feel bad if you tell the kid to leave you alone. You are working. If they persist, seek out the bride or groom, or whoever is running the show (often it is the emcee, or a close friend of the bride or groom, or the "persons of honor", who have accepted the responsibility to run the party). Just tell them what's going on and state (politely but firmly) that you don't want the child to harm himself or break anything.

In most cases, the person in charge will be horrified and rush the child from the scene. If not, make sure that you have a clause in your contract that states that if anything is broken at the gig by any of the guests, the client will assume liability. If that is too harsh, then you can collect a damage deposit which is refundable after the event. If little Jenny spills cola on your speakers, at least you can keep the deposit. Also, make sure that you buy insurance for your equipment, because it just might be you that spills the drink all over your keyboard!

Problem: Aggressive Or Drunk Customers

It doesn't really matter what type of party you are DJing—weddings, barbeques, proms, or a community event—most of the time there is going to be drinking and lots of it. People go to parties to let their hair down and have a good time. This means, for many people, excessive drinking and partying. This may also mean, unfortunately for you, that people are going to get more aggressive as the alcohol lessens their inhibitions.

Make sure to do a little research before you DJ the event. If the event is at a community hall, golf & country club hall, or hotel ballroom, make sure to know who the person in charge of the hall is. Remember, this might not be the same person who is actually paying you for your night's work. The bride & groom's parents may be footing the bill for the wedding reception, but the hotel security chief is probably sitting at the front desk of the hotel lobby.

Also, make sure that you know where the exits are. This may sound strange, but you never know when some weird event may happen, like a fight breaking out, or a fire may erupt. Lights are low, music is loud and people are drunk. All sorts of weird things can—and do—happen.

If you do happen to get into an argument or an incident with a person at the party, try to handle it yourself. But if they are being unreasonable, you are perfectly within your right to go to the client and ask them to handle one of their rowdy guests. It may be "old uncle Stuart" who gets drunk at every party and tries to get in a fight, or some other weird relative that the client knows. The bottom line is, the client invited these people, and if there is a problem, they probably want to know about it. Remember, you and your client have the same goal: to put on a great party and that includes great music. In order for you to do your job well, you need to be free from being bothered by unruly guests.

Problem: The "Know-It-All"

This was me when I hired a DJ in the mid-1990s. We went in to visit the local DJ in town and I presented him with a list of 100 songs that I wanted played at my event—and in a specific order to boot! I had spent the previous evening detailing out *exactly* what songs would be played and when. I had the whole evening already played out in my mind—when I think about it now, I shudder. How could I possibly know what songs would work over a four-hour period? Even the DJ doesn't know that!

At the time, I didn't understand what a DJ actually did. I had no concept that what I liked would not necessarily be enjoyed by other people at the party. I didn't realize that there would be lots of seniors there, or that not everyone had grown up listening to a certain radio station in town. (Some people at the event were even from other countries!) Anne Murray? No way! Neil Diamond? Laughable! What do you mean that other people, people I invited, would request *their own* songs?

The DJ flat out told me that he would not play the list. He was totally polite and understanding, and explained to me that while the songs that I had on the list were quite good, they were not songs that should be played with a mixed group of people, many different age groups, cultures and geographic origins. "If you want to have a horrible event," he told me, "then play these songs. Otherwise, let me do my thing and you will have a rocking party".

It was a lesson learned for me, and for what it was worth, the DJ at the event was terrific. He played a few of the bands that I wanted, but to tell you the truth, he did a much better job at filling the dance floor than my songs would have.

People hire a DJ to play songs, take requests and engineer the party. If a potential client gives you a list of songs to play, take the list and play the songs that you agree with. However, many songs that are "awesome" by the client's standards just won't play well on a dance floor. These would include many "radio" songs that are not dance songs and not ballads. They may sound great in the stereo or at work in the office, but they won't fly on the dance floor. If you ask any ten people on the street about their all-time favorite songs, you are going to get ten completely different set lists.

For example, look at the songs that are always smash hits at weddings—Boney M's *Rasputin*, Chubby Checker's *The Twist* and Kenny Loggin's *Footloose*. These songs just don't get on the mainstream radio stations all that often. You wouldn't normally play them while relaxing and enjoying a book on the sofa. However, when played loud at a dance, they are amazing crowd pleasers.

If the client still insists that you play the songs in a specific order, or that you only play songs on a pre-determined list, then be prepared to walk away. An event like this is a guaranteed loser for you and the client—don't waste your time and money on an impossible task. After all, if they want a jukebox, they can rent one (or simply plug a laptop into a speaker system).

Your Image

How you look will depend on what types of music you are playing and what types of gigs you are performing at. Remember, you will be noticed by hundreds of people at your gig. Even if the lights are turned down low and all of the spotlights are focused on the dance floor, people are still going to wonder who is playing the music. And, of course, people are going to see you when you go get a drink, take requests, or hang out at the event.

What is too stodgy? What is unprofessional? These are tough questions. The best piece of advice is also somewhat vague: dress appropriately for the event. If it is a wedding, then definitely a suit and tie (or a business dress) is appropriate. If it's a country & western gig, then usually jeans and a plaid shirt will work. You might even want to bring a back-up set of clothes with you and keep it in your vehicle. That way, if you do show up and you are not dressed appropriately, you can "formal up" in the bathroom quickly and not sit around wondering if people are giving you the hairy eyeball.

For a DJ who plays house music in a club, you should be sporting hip clothes that are current. Ask yourself, what would the audience normally buy and wear? In these cases, you probably don't want to stand out and "look too professional", so it's best to be one of the gang and dress with the latest trends.

Club DJs and bar DJs are radically different than corporate gigs. In the bar or club, you will want to have a slick image. In these cases, you are literally the performer and so you will want to dress more like a star.

Chapter 4:
DJ Software

The internet is an amazing place. Type in "DJ" or "deejay" into any online search engine and you can spend the rest of your life looking at other businesses, tips, ideas, and opinions about the industry. One of the great things about the internet is that it is free and unregulated—no one owns the internet—and as such, free speech reigns.

That, unfortunately, can also be the downside to the internet. There is so much stuff online that it can be difficult to find real information among the thousands of blogs, advertisements, opinions and rants. However, that is why you bought this book! I have a few cool sites that will help out any aspiring DJ, and we start with the fundamental equipment that any good DJ needs: software.

Before You Start

There are many different ways to DJ. You can have a pile of CDs and play them through double-turntables. You can use cassette tapes, or vinyl, or digital mp3s, or any combination of the above. The system I am going to describe involves digital mp3s. Here's the basic process:

1. Take your CD and copy it into your computer using your music software. Create mp3s files from your CD. You can also

just purchase the music from iTunes, or any of the hundreds of music sites that are out there.

2. Organize your mp3 files into directories so that you can access them easily.

3. Using DJ software, play them through your DJ equipment (speaker system).

You don't need a super-duper great computer, although you should have a good CD-ROM drive, at least a couple of gigabytes of hard disk space, and enough RAM memory to play the songs without any skipping or errors. When you copy the songs into your computer, make sure to copy them on a medium or high-quality setting. Doing this will create larger files, and thus take up more space on your computer, but it will be worth it. You should have enough hard drive space to have at least 1,000 songs. To DJ with confidence, you should have the goal of having at least a thousand songs on your computer.

Every new computer these days comes with "ripping" software, which is the term that is coined to turn your CD song into an mp3 file. The term "mp3" stands for MPEG Audio Layer 3, which is a type of file that is much smaller than the previous sound files (like WAV files) that took up huge amounts of hard drive space. Mp3s are smaller and yet they still sound great. An mp3 file, if recorded properly, should sound just as good as the original in the CD.

What About My iPod / iPad / Tablet?

You might be able to completely DJ a gig using only an iPad, or iPod, or even an iPhone. If you can do that, then great! The only downside to this is that you may not have the capability to play a CD. There have been times when someone at a dance will literally run out to their car in a dress, only to reappear minutes later, out of breath and anxious that you play their track from their CD.

You definitely can say no in this case, but there are times when you may want a backup system in place just in case there is a problem or special request.

Copyright Issues

What is a "copyright"? Not surprisingly, this can be one of the most confusing areas of law, because the digital age has produced a whole generation of people who have used the internet and computer technology to create illegal copies of music. Also, the law is constantly changing and as such there are many myths about what is allowed and what is illegal.

Basically, a copyright is a form of protection provided by the law. The author of an "original work" is protected. An "original work" may be literary, like a book, an essay, or a poem; dramatic, such as a screenplay or commercial; musical, like a recording (CD or digital file) or even just a song. It could even be artistic (like a painting or sculpture).

This protection is available to both published and unpublished works. Copyright occurs at the moment you have created the work. It doesn't have to be "published" like a Stephen King best-seller. Your personal manuscript that is sitting in your nightstand? That is copyrighted. That song that you wrote back in grade 5 and now sits on one of your old cassette tapes? Copyrighted.

Copyright law generally gives the owner of copyright the exclusive right to reproduce the work, distribute copies of that work, or perform the work in public. For DJs, this means that the copyright holder has the exclusive right to publicly transmit and perform the recording digitally. It also gives the copyright owner the exclusive right to authorize others to do these acts.

For music, often the copyright holder is the songwriter, although sometimes people sell their copyright to others. A notable example of this would be Michael Jackson when he purchased the rights to many Beatles songs. Suddenly Beatles tunes were popping up in commercials on television... whether Paul McCartney or any of the other Beatles liked it or not. McCartney had sold the copyright for some of his songs, and he no longer had any say over where and how they could be used.

If you buy a CD, it doesn't mean that you own the copyrights to that music. You have only purchased the rights to that particular copy. That means that you cannot create a copy of the CD to perform in public places such as a bar, dance club, or community hall—but does that mean that you cannot play any top hits as a DJ? Fortunately, there is SOCAN in Canada and ASCAP in the United States.

SOCAN (Canada)

The Society of Composers, Authors, and Music Publishers of Canada (known as SOCAN) is the only nationwide performance rights organization in Canada. They are a non-profit organization that represents composers, artists, performers, songwriters and publishers of musical works from Canada and around the world.

Check out this organization at www.socan.ca. They have a comprehensive website that details copyrights, tariffs and the industry in general. Here are a few of the basics:

- *A performing right* is the right to perform music works in public. It also includes communicating music to the public by telecommunication.(like a public address system in a mall, or over the phone). It is one of the rights granted to creators of copyright-protected works under the Copyright Act of Canada. SOCAN acts on behalf of its members so that they can administer the fees and tariffs for them.

- *A performing right license* allows you to perform any of the musical works in SOCAN's repertoire in public. Without it, you would have to get permission from every songwriter, composer, lyricist and music publisher for every piece of music you play or perform. A SOCAN license is the simplest way to allow you access to virtually the world's entire repertoire of copyright-protected music.

SOCAN collects license fees and takes into account its operating costs. It distributes the net revenue as royalties to its members, who are the songwriters, lyricists and composers, as well as the publishers. There are also affiliated international societies for many of these people as well.

How much does this cost and who pays? Well, the amount owed to SOCAN varies by event. There are a number of different tariffs, and they are laid out on their website. Check back once a year to see if anything changes on an annual basis. Currently, the tariff for a "reception, convention, assembly or fashion show" can range from about twenty dollars to about one hundred dollars without dancing, all the way up to two hundred dollars with dancing.

The great news is that for the DJ, this has little to no impact whatsoever. It is important to note that the *owner and operator of a venue using any live music, live or recorded, is responsible for obtaining the appropriate SOCAN music licenses and paying the appropriate fees.* This means that as a DJ for a wedding, reception, party, or most events, you are a hired consultant or entertainer, and not the host of the venue.

You would pay SOCAN if you were running a party and hosting the event. An example of this would be putting on your own concert and hiring a band. In this case, you are the promoter and are running the show. If you choose to DJ your own event, then you would, as the promoter, pay the SOCAN fees.

You cannot make the client pay SOCAN. All you can do in this instance is read up on the rules of Canadian copyright, take a look at the SOCAN website, and note that you should pay tariffs if you are the promoter (not the DJ, who is hired by the promoter).

ASCAP (United States)

The American Society of Composers, Authors and Publishers (also known as ASCAP) is a group that was formed to make sure that people who are playing copyrighted songs are paid accordingly. If you are a songwriter, you can become a member and then participate in a royalty structure—in effect, you can get paid if someone plays your work in public.

The ASCAP website (www.ascap.com) is quite comprehensive and covers much more than just DJing or playing at a bar. Take the time to read through it (if you are American) and learn your rights and responsibilities.

For a DJ, the big question is "do I need to buy an ASCAP license in order to play Michael Jackson, Madonna or any other CDs or mp3 music?" The short answer is that it depends on whose event it is.

If you are hired to play an event, than it is the responsibility of the business owner or promoter to obtain a license. This means that the DJ is just a "hired hand" who shows up and plays songs. Since it is the event promoter (or business owner) who is deemed to obtain the ultimate benefit from the DJs performance, the event promoter or business owner is responsible for getting a license.

If you are DJ and you are hosting your own event, however, then you are responsible. What is your own event? Well, if you rent the hall, put up posters advertising your Halloween party, and you pay all the expenses and collect all the ticket revenue, then that is your venue. If you show up and play a wedding, and you are handed a cheque for a few hundred dollars, then the wedding party is ultimately responsible for obtaining a license.

To Buy Or Not To Buy

You don't need to spend a lot of money on software. In fact, to start out, you don't need to pay for software at all. I found a few programs on the internet and I was able to download them and use them for free. These programs are designed and built by people who love DJing and want to share their talent with the world. The software is 100% free and 100% legal. If you are using an Apple computer or iPad, there are "apps" out there that can do the job of mixing and fading. Sometimes these apps are free; other times they may only cost a few dollars and it can be well worth it to purchase them.

Freeware is a term that has been bantered about; it basically means free software that has been given away to the public. Sometimes the author or programmer will ask the user to consider a voluntary donation if you really like the software. There is also *shareware*, which is a term that describes software that is available for free, but often has a trial period (like 30 or 60 days). After the trial period, the program won't work, and the user must either purchase the full version, or stop using the software. Sometimes you can get shareware versions of software, but some of the features have been disabled. The idea here is that you try the program, and if you like it, you purchase the full version.

Remember this rule: *use software that is reliable and comfortable for you.*

Don't try out new software at a gig—do it at home when you are running through your songs to see what you like and don't like about a program. If you really like a certain DJ program, stick with it for gigs and try other stuff out in your spare time. Don't get caught off guard at a gig because you didn't know how to use your software.

The best way to become acquainted with DJ software is to visit some sites that have different DJ programs, download them, and try them out. There are lots of different "free software" websites out there. I have used www.download.com quite a bit, but there are many others, such as www.freewarefiles.com. You can just type in "free software" in a search engine and see what comes up. Here are two examples of a few programs that I have used and enjoy.

MixVibes

There is a lot to see and hear at www.mixvibes.com. They offer a "pro" version of their software, but check out the free version first and see if you like it.

The freeware version of MixVibes is very basic and should give you a great starting point. Basically, it allows you to play an mp3 track in one line while loading up another track in the second line. Why is this a big deal?

For some gigs, it won't be. You can just play a bunch of songs in a pre-set order and walk away. Indeed, some parties have exactly that—the people running the show just put in a mix CD or a play list and then let it run. So why do people even want a DJ at their gig?

The answer is that the DJ can adjust to the requests and flow of the party. For example, a DJ can take requests and insert a "special" song within a very short timeframe. A mix CD can't do that—you just have to patiently wait for your track to show up or wait until a new CD is played. A DJ can also sense if the crowd is getting tired and is in the mood for a slower song. Alternatively, a DJ can sense a crowd that is getting restless, and can switch up tracks to bring in more dance-friendly, upbeat music. A DJ is a living, breathing jukebox who can feel the crowd.

With MixVibes, you can load up a second track while the first one is playing. The other cool thing that you can do is overlap tracks. Have you noticed that some songs have a long "fade out" at the end? Sometimes a rocking song can slowly fade out, and these periods can be long—sometimes 30 seconds or so. If the track were on a mix CD or just allowed to run, the crowd would have 15-30 seconds of "dead time"— time that is spent standing around looking foolish instead of dancing. A DJ can start up the next track right when the first one is starting to fade out. In fact, some DJs can work it so that there is a continuous flow of music all night, without any fade outs.

An example of "MixVibes" digital software. Note the two players (one on the left, another on the right) for digital files.

The next time you listen to the radio, listen with a DJ's ear. Have you noticed that a DJ on the radio will talk over an opening to a song? There might be a 20-second instrumental opening, but the DJ will talk about the weather, an upcoming concert, or anything... right up until the moment that the singer starts singing the song. Although I would not recommend blabbing over songs at a wedding or party, the idea is the same—that you want to keep the music flowing smoothly, with little or no "soft air" or "dead air". Have one song come in while another song is fading out. Indeed, often the DJ will cut to another song as soon as the song begins to fade out. A three-minute song could be very long in the DJ world.

VU Player

VU Player is a simple, lightweight music player that is free to use. It is an alternative to the heavier software that often accompanies newer computers. VU Player just plays audio files, such as mp3 or wav, and lets you shuffle them around, load them up and create play lists, all without a significant drain on your computer.

If you computer is running a program that takes up a lot of memory, it could run at or near full capacity. This means that the tracks might skip or hiccup when you play them. VU Player is good because it can consistently play tracks without skipping, which is definitely a good thing when the speakers are on loud! This is a great program if you have an older computer—there are no bells or whistles, but the program is very easy to use and it does not use up much computer power.

VU Player is found online at www.vuplayer.com. It doesn't just play mp3s; like many media players, it handles all sorts of media files, like mod, wav, wma and CD files.

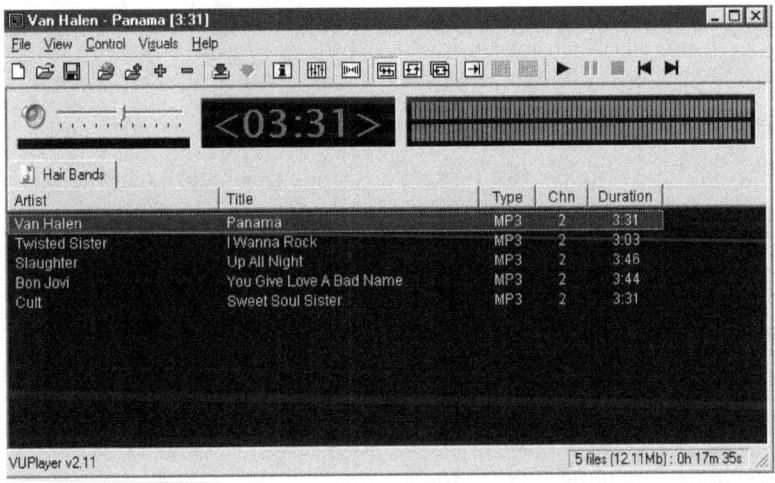

VU Player is a reliable, simple and lightweight tool for playing media files.

There are literally hundreds of different types of DJ-media software programs out there, ranging from simple media players to high-end, professional beat-mixing packages. Some of them are very expensive, ranging in the hundreds of dollars. Make sure to download and use the trial version before purchasing anything expensive. Or, you may find that the free versions are good enough for you and your needs.

Creating mp3 Files

The easiest way to create and play media files is to use a "jukebox" program or an audio program on your computer. Virtually every new computer comes with audio software, as this is a main selling feature of many laptops and desktop computers.

You can find free ones online. Check out websites like www.download.com or just type on "freeware" or "freeware mp3" using a search engine like *Yahoo!, Webcrawler* or of course *Google.*

You can adjust the settings in these programs to make either high-quality or lower-quality mp3s. If you have the space on your computer, make the highest-quality mp3s you can. Remember, these mp3s will be played loudly through DJ equipment, so you want to minimize any lower-quality attributes like hissing or skipping, which sometimes happens when you make a copy of an audio file. Although the higher-quality files take up more room, hopefully your computer will be used only for your DJ business and as such should have plenty of room. A standard laptop with 10 gigabytes of memory can easily hold 5,000 songs, for example, provided that you aren't filling up the hard drives with movies, pictures, and computer games.

Make sure to play, in advance of a gig, every single audio file that you create. Do this at home, well in advance of the event. Sometimes errors occur during the recording process, and you should know ahead of time if the song doesn't record properly. Don't wait for the gig to discover that the couple's wedding song has the last twenty seconds cut off, or the intro is beeping and skipping because of a greasy fingerprint on the original CD.

Some of the better computer software programs have advanced options like "fading out" a track early. Some dance songs are really great, but run over six minutes long—often too long during a wedding reception. Any song, no matter how great, should not be longer than five minutes if you can help it. (There are a few notable exceptions, like Led Zeppelin's "Stairway to Heaven" or the Beatles "Hey Jude"). If you can "fade out" the song after 5 minutes, go for it and keep the variety strong during your gig.

You should have a minimum of 1,000 songs in your arsenal before you actually DJ your first gig. It is critical that you are able to find your songs quickly and effortlessly during the event. Here's an example of just one way that you can arrange them on your computer:

1 – Classic Rock

2 – Modern Rock

3 – Country Fast

4 – Country Ballad

5 – Rap

6 – Dinner Music / Classical

7 – Brand-New Chart Toppers

8 – Disco

9 - Wedding

10 – Halloween

11 – Christmas

12 - Sound effects, theme music

This is just an example—of course you can organize them any way you like. You could have one huge folder, with every band and every song in it, and just alphabetize it. If you are comfortable with that, then that is great. Other DJs have each band in its own folder, with all of their respective songs in each folder for easy access.

When recording your mp3 files, make sure to have the band name and the track name on there. This is especially helpful if you want to search for a song but don't know or can't remember the name of it, or who sings it. What was the name of that INXS track? Search for all tracks with "INXS" in the title and it should come up.

The best way to learn how to do this is to spend a day and fool around on your computer. Download some free programs and give them a try. If you don't like them, uninstall them and move on to the next one.

Creating 1,000 mp3 files is hard work and will take some time. Once you get 1,000 songs in your computer, make sure to back up your files, as you should be doing anyway on your computer. Burn your inventory to blank CD-R discs (recordable CDs) and then store them in a box. If you have any downloaded programs, back those up as well. This way, if your computer decides to die, you can at least have all of your mp3 files on hand (not to mention your software applications, copies of contracts, spreadsheets containing your business information, and the like). Don't learn this the hard way—spend an afternoon and back up your stuff. It is time well spent.

Name ▲	Size	Type
📁 01 - Client Specific		File Folder
📁 02 - R&B Songs		File Folder
📁 03 - Ballads		File Folder
📁 04 - Oldies		File Folder
📁 05 - Novelty		File Folder
📁 06 - Classical		File Folder
📁 07 - Christmas		File Folder
📁 08 - Heavy Metal		File Folder
📁 09 - Top 40		File Folder
📁 10 - Electronica		File Folder

An example of one of the many ways that you can organize your songs on a computer. There is no right way—it is only important that you know where the songs are located.

To Remix Or Not To Remix

How much is "too much of a good thing"? Some people love dance remixes of popular songs. Others hate them and just want to hear the original "radio" version.

Unusually, dance remixes are longer and retain the general words and structure of the original song, but have "extras" such as extended drums, heavy bass, remixed instruments, or different grooves. As such, the song can sound radically different from the original. Sometimes DJs will mash two completely different songs together to create a whole new song. I heard Outkast's "Hey Ya" and Queen's "We Will Rock You" mixed together. Some people love this stuff, and others don't.

If in doubt, play the original. If the song is a popular single, then you really can't go wrong. After all, if it is popular, then lots of people will have heard it and will want to dance to it. Dances are usually not the place to learn about new songs; most people just want to dance to songs that they already know and love.

Using dance remixes depend primarily on the venue and the audience. If you are in a club or a bar, then usually dance remixes are more accepted and welcomed. However, for standard corporate parties or weddings, most people love the classics and don't want to stop halfway through a song and ask "wait a minute, do I know this one?".

The most important thing to remember about selecting music and creating a valuable catalog is to listen to lots of different types of music. When you are in the car, for example, flip around on the radio stations instead of just playing your favorite CD. Take out different CDs from the library or swap with some friends. Remember, you need to know about different types of music if you want to be on the cutting edge, and if you are a professional, you need to treat your passion for music like work, with dedicated hours to your craft.

The Club DJ: Remixing With Software

This book is basically describing two different types of DJing: corporate gigs, which normally showcase radio-friendly songs, and club gigs, which feature wild remixes and dance tracks that are new and fresh. These are two totally different types of events, and what is suitable for one might be totally unacceptable in the other.

For club DJs, for example, if you played a retro 1980s track without any remixing, you might get a bored audience who would abandon the dance floor. However, if you played a dance-remix of a hot Latin track at the insurance company Christmas party, you might wind up being the talk of the office for the next year (and not in a good way).

For club DJs, you will want to work on remixing, editing songs, beat mixing and beat matching. The goal of the club DJ is to create a seamless flow of music that runs continuously. A great example of DJ beat matching and beat mixing are the *MuchDance* series of CDs that are available in Canada. Professional remixers have taken radio songs and merged them all together into one long, seamless track. If you play a MuchDance CD, you will notice that there are no spaces in between the songs. This is what the club DJ is trying to accomplish—the morphing from one song into another.

Getting Started: Audio Editing Software

If you want to try this sort of remixing, but don't want to spend hundreds of dollars on professional-grade audio software, that is okay. There is a free, open-source software package available on the internet. It can be a great tool for the novice DJ who is looking to experiment with beat mixing, matching songs and splicing up sounds.

The program is called *Audacity*, and it is available for free online. The official website is located at www.audacity.sourceforge.net. Audacity is "open source", which means that the code for Audacity is available to anyone who wants it. Not only is it freeware, but because it is open source, the actual code for the program is available to anyone who wants to modify it, add tools and features, or otherwise build on it.

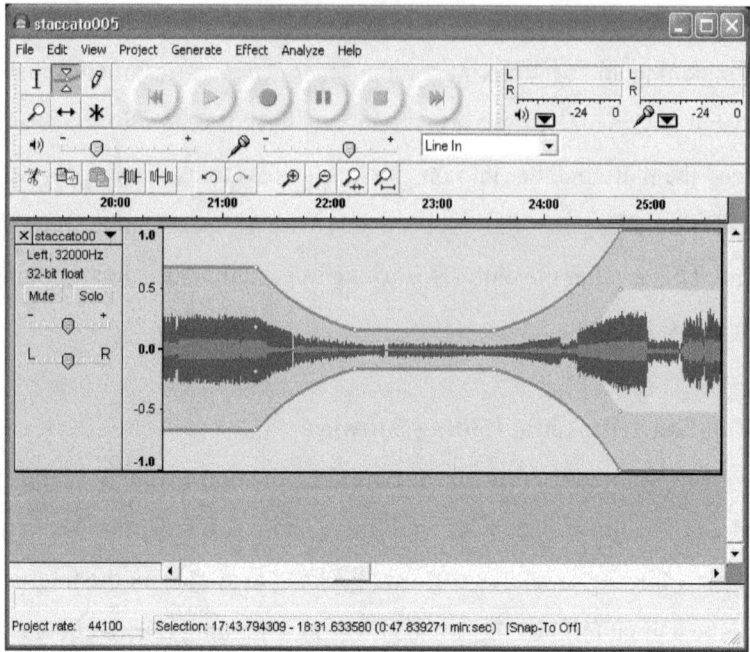

The Audacity software allows users to edit, clip and merge different sounds together to create something completely different.

You can do all sorts of neat things with Audacity, such as record live audio, convert tapes and old vinyl into digital recordings or CDs, edit different sound files, and even change the speed or pitch of a recording. You can edit, mix, splice and merge songs together. Using Audacity, you can add echo or different sounds effects right into a song, or even play it in reverse. The best part is that you can save your project and play it at a later date.

As mentioned, Audacity is completely free. It was written by a group of volunteers and distributed under the GNU General Public License (GPL). Because it is open-source code, there are frequent updates and add-ons by users.

Audacity is just one of many different software applications that are free and available online. Another one, for example, is called *Wavesurfer* and is available from the Royal Institute of Technology (KTH), Department of Speech, Music and Hearing Institutionen för Tal, Musik och Hörsel in Stockholm, Sweden. You can get it for free at www.speech.kth.se/wavesurfer. Again, these are just a couple of examples of many free software applications that you can use to edit your software.

The best way to familiarize yourself with them is to download them and give them a try. Try free first; if it doesn't suit your needs, go for something that costs money. Reliability is 90 per cent of success. It doesn't matter how many bells and whistles it has at first—make sure when you press play, some high-quality music comes out.

Chapter 5:
DJ Hardware

What good are software and mp3 files if you have nothing to play it on? A good quality computer, speakers, mixer and ancillaries are key to becoming a good, reliable DJ. There's no sense in having all sorts of tricks up your sleeves, like smoke bombs, lights, strobes and beat mixing, if your computer crashes, your speakers crackle and no one can understand what you are saying through your cheap microphone. The only thing worse than doing a below-average job is doing that same job in front of a huge throng of people.

Before you buy anything, take a weekend and visit two, three or four music stores. Check out speakers. Compare prices and power. There are incredibly high-end speakers and audio systems out there, but they may be not only super-expensive, but way more powerful than what you will ever need.

Remember this rule concerning hardware: *buy new and look after your equipment.*

What sort of gigs do you anticipate on playing? How many people will be at these functions? Weddings, community events and school dances will seldom have more than a couple of hundred people at them. This means that you don't need 5 huge speakers and an amplifier capable of rocking a professional sports-sized arena. After all, the DJ business is supposed to be profitable, and that means getting good quality equipment for a reasonable price.

It never ceases to amaze me when I watch bands play at local pubs and their equipment is all ratty and beat up. There's no excuse for this, unless they bought it that way. Don't buy second-hand equipment. The equipment may seem like a "great deal" until it blows up. You should be able to find good speakers, a mixer and a computer for under $2,000 if you shop around.

If you are not interested in buying your equipment, or if the thought of investing $2,000 in professional DJ equipment is too scary, then consider renting. Many music stores offer DJ packages for rental. You should be able to grab a basic set of speakers, a mixer and some CD turntables for around $150 for an evening. If you are charging $300 or more for the gig, then you will still be making some good money, and you won't have to store the equipment. Shop around and compare costs. You may find that a low-priced rental arrangement would be more convenient, at least at the start. However, if you want to be a professional DJ on a long-term basis, it makes fiscal sense to purchase some high-end gear that will last you a long time.

Let's take a closer look at DJ hardware: the computer, speakers, amplifier / mixer, and ancillary stuff.

The Computer

The computer industry has been changing and evolving for the past twenty years, and it would appear that more changes are in the works as more and more people are "going digital"—high-quality cameras, crystal-clear music, e-mail and the internet are playing a larger and larger role in our everyday lives. Hard disk memory, RAM, and CPU (computer processing unit) speed are all increasing, it would seem, at mind-boggling frequency. People are often wary to buy a high-end computer because a month later their expensive purchase is obsolete.

The good news is that you have a basic set of minimum requirements in order to DJ with digital files using a computer. Once those are met, you simply do not need to upgrade—ever. You might want to, but you won't need to. Remember the difference. With a personal computer, you might upgrade if you want to play the latest games, or use the best software, or try something new that your existing computer can't handle. However, with your DJ computer, you will be playing the same files (or type of files) with the same software for a long, long time. You will be using specialized software, and your computer, if it is used for DJing, will become specialized hardware. The only time that you might want to upgrade is if your computer is crashing, you start experiencing problems (like songs skipping for no reason) or other performance issues (like needing more hard disk space to store even more songs). Otherwise, buy a basic computer for your DJ business and let other people sweat about upgrades and having their computer become obsolete.

The key here is remembering the basics—just get a basic laptop or desktop computer that is capable of playing mp3 files to start out. Your iPad or MacBook might work just fine as well. A good quality laptop will come with a CD-ROM drive, a mouse or touch pad, and enough hard disk memory and CPU power to run mp3 songs no problem. You should be able to find the basic model for about $1,000 U.S., or cheaper if you buy an older, used model.

Another good habit to get into is to have your DJ computer be exactly that—the computer that you use to DJ with. Don't put computer games, other software programs or pictures on your DJ computer. Use it exclusively for DJing. Every time that you install a program or uninstall a program, it affects the computer. As any good IT person knows, a program never truly "uninstalls"—there are always a couple of files that somehow seem to stay in your computer. Why change your computer's registry by adding files or changing things around? Keep the computer clean and use it for DJing only to avoid potential problems.

Here's the bare essentials to running mp3 software on a laptop or desktop computer:

- Hard disk space: Most new computers come with 10, 20 or even 50 gigabytes of hard disk space. You should have enough room on your hard drive for thousands upon thousands of songs. Even an older computer with 1 gigabyte of space would hold almost a thousand songs (depending, of course, on the quality / size of files). A typical medium to high-quality mp3 file takes up about 3 to 4 megabytes (there are 1,000 megabytes in a gigabyte). This means that you should be able to store 300 to 400 songs if you have one gigabyte of memory. You should strive for at least 1,000 songs in your database, but more is better.

- MHZ (megahertz) of power: This totally depends on the requirements of the software that you are playing. For lower-end freeware, virtually any Pentium-level computer or higher should be able to play the mp3 tracks without skipping or freezing. Most new computers come with a gigahertz or higher of processing power, which is much more than needed. Most new computers are designed to play all sorts of media files, like DVDs and movie clips, which by definition have both audio and visual components. Since you are DJing, you are just interested in the audio component to start out.

- <u>Mouse:</u> I originally used a desktop computer to DJ, but the business eventually upgraded to a basic laptop and I enjoyed the change. The laptop is much easier to set up and it came with increased processing power and speed. If you do go with a laptop, make sure to purchase a mouse (which is usually a few dollars extra). Although laptops come with a "mouse pad" on the computer, the mouse with a cord is much easier to use. With the lights down and the music up, you need to run smoothly.

- <u>CD player:</u> Virtually all new computers come with a CD-ROM drive, which is a drive capable of playing CDs. Many computers come with a DVD drive, and these play CDs as well. There might be special cases where you need to play a CD track off of the CD itself, as opposed to playing the recorded mp3 file. I would recommend getting a CD burner as well, which is very helpful to back up your files—and not just your mp3 files. It is a good idea to burn your contents of your computer onto a few CD-Rs once a year, so that if your computer crashes, you have backup copies of your important data. Anyone who has ever suffered through a computer virus or a computer crash knows how devastating this sort of unplanned event can be.

Speakers

What kind of speakers do you need? How big should they be? Is two going to be enough? I had visions of cranking up my mp3s at my first DJ gig and not having enough power to be heard—or worse, having too much juice coming from the computer and mixer and wrecking my speakers. However, a little research should alleviate these fears and have you excited about turning up the volume!

There are different types of speakers that produce different types of sounds. The speakers that reproduce sounds that are in the lowest part of the audio spectrum are called *woofers* or *sub-woofers*. These help produce the bass sounds and the lower-sounding parts of a song. Tweeters help reproduce the higher-end parts of a song, such as drum symbols or high guitar licks. The parts in-between the high-end and the low-end parts of a song fall in the middle, and these are reproduced by the mid-range speakers. Some speakers are designed to handle all of the above, and they are called full-range speakers. They operate like all-season tires; while they don't specialize in winter conditions or summer conditions, you can drive in them all year round. Full-range speakers aren't specifically designed to specialize in the high or low-end parts of songs, but they will play all parts reasonably well.

Don't get overwhelmed by all of the speaker choices out there—to start out, you should get two high-quality, full-range speakers. If you want to compliment your package later by purchasing a woofer or a tweeter, that is a long-term decision.

But what exactly is "high quality"? That is a subjective term. The important thing to remember when pricing out speakers is to make sure that they will play your music loudly and clearly.

Speaker wattage is one of the most confusing and frustrating things when starting out in the DJ business. Will four speakers be more powerful than two? Not necessarily—it depends on the type of speaker and the amplifier. Check out this typical post that I pieced together from different DJ forums online:

> My speaker specs at 8 ohms are 150 watts RMS and 300 watts peak power. How does that correspond to amp specs? For example, the QSX 1450 says it pushes 280 watts at 8 ohms per channel. So does that mean I will get 140 watts to each speaker (which are two on each channel)? What number should I be working with from the speakers, 150 RMS or 300 Peak? I want to get the best amp that will push the most to my speakers without hurting them. I need to understand what my particular speaker can handle from an amp. Again, the model is a MTX TP112. Thanks...

Yikes! That would scare off most aspiring DJs. Do you need a degree in cybernetics or engineering to hook up speakers and maximize your output? Not really. For the beginner, don't worry about those types of details. Here's the very basic information that you need to purchase and set up speakers.

Wattage is a term that roughly translates in to electrical power. However, just because a speaker has a higher wattage, that doesn't necessarily mean that it will sound better or play louder. Another characteristic to look at when checking out speakers is the "sensitivity specification". This means that a speaker might have different ratings for how much sound comes out for the amount of input that is put through a speaker.

Speakers that are very powerful usually have lower sensitivity numbers. Speakers with the highest sensitivity numbers typically can't handle as much power. This makes sense, as many speakers are designed for specific purposes. For DJing, you want basic sound that is going to be played loud, compared to a smaller speaker designed for a home theater system, for example. It is rare to find a speaker than can handle both high power and high sensitivity rating (especially for a low price). Really powerful (industrial grade) amplifiers can be really costly, so speakers that are more efficient (that is, speakers that can generate more sound with a smaller input) are generally desired so long as you are satisfied with the sound.

To put it another way: get efficient speakers—ones with middle-of-the-road power and sensitivity training. Remember the "all-season" tires—you want something that can handle everything, without specializing in any one thing.

Try out the speakers at the sound stores that you visit. Take your laptop to the stores and plug your computer into the speakers (obviously ask the store owner if this is okay in advance). Most sales people at music stores love to help out new customers and will be happy to let you test out a system. If they are not helpful, go on to the next store. If you are dropping $1,000 on speakers and amplifiers, take your time and do it right.

Basic DJ speakers that you can use as a guide would be two 150-watt speakers, which is exactly what I purchased when I was starting out.

For the DJ business, I bought two speakers—150 watts continuous, 300 watts program and 600 watts peak. "Continuous" means that you can play at that level consistently for a long period of time (like a full DJ gig). The "peak" wattage is the maximum that you can burst out of your speakers for a really short time (a couple of seconds) if you have to. The "program" watts refers to the capabilities of the speakers to handle "real world" music, and all of the peaks and valleys therein. These two speakers can handle a gig where a couple of hundred people would gather (like a community hall, church, or country club) no problem.

Amplifiers / Mixers

If you thought speakers were confusing and mysterious, you are not alone. The mystery continues into the world amplifiers, where you can spend the rest of your life looking at the hundreds of available combinations of speakers and amplifiers.

Basically, you need something that connects your computer to your speakers. You can't just plug two professional 150-watt DJ speakers into your laptop. Your computer has a little tiny hole in the back or side that is designed for headphones. That is the only exit for the music to travel from your computer to the hundreds of dancers at the big party.

An amplifier or mixer is the "in-between" part that takes your output from the computer and makes the sound bigger. When I first started out, I was able to find a 100-watt amplifier that had 4 channels in the front and two outputs in the back. The inputs in the front are for the computer, the microphones, and two other devices (which you probably won't use) and the two outputs in the back connect to the two 150-watt speakers previously mentioned.

You could use a 2-channel mixer if you can find one, although I saw 4 channels as the minimum in most cases. Here is why a mixer is cool: each of the four channels has its own volume settings, so you can turn off channel one (the microphone) and turn up the volume on channel two (the computer, or music). If someone wants to speak at the party, you simply turn down the computer channel and turn up the microphone channel. There are easy-to-use dials on the front of the mixer and you can just twist the knobs instantly.

The channels on the mixer also have tone settings in most cases as well, and some have equalizer settings, like treble, bass, reverb, and others. The mixer will also have a "master volume" that affects all of the channels at once. If you want to turn everything up or down, you can use the master volume.

Mixers are often used by rock bands. You could put a guitar in channel one, for example, and then connect a bass in channel two, a microphone in channel three, and a microphone for the drummer in channel four, just as an example. The output would go into a recording device and you could tweak the individual settings of each musician so that you get the desired effect that you are looking for (you could tone down the drums, for example, which is typically louder than the other instruments, or increase the bass if that was your inclination).

Mixers are useful tools, but you typically won't be using multiple channels at the same time like a band would. Instead, to start out, you just need to hook up the microphone to one channel, the computer (your music source) to the second channel, and then use one at a time. You might, on occasion, want to just turn down the music channel and talk over the music using the microphone. This is typical during "party songs" such as musical chairs or conga lines, where the DJ coaxes the crowd as the music plays. Using a mixer enables the DJ to talk while the music plays, just like at a radio station.

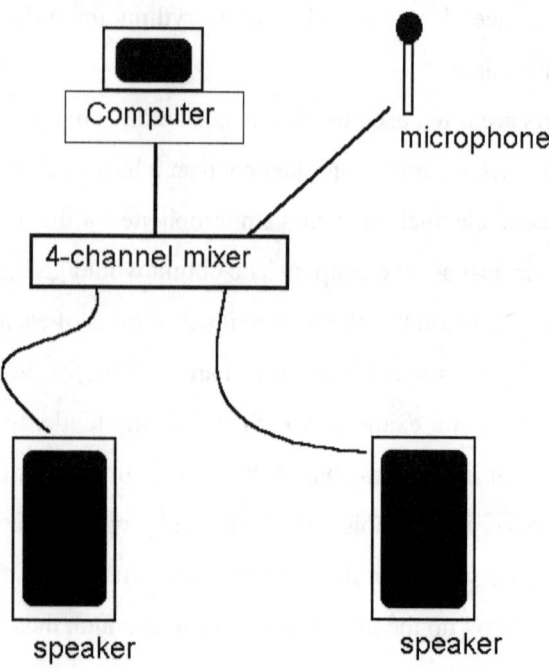

A typical, simple DJ setup. The computer and microphone feed into the 4-channel mixer (only two channels are being used in this example). The mixer amplifies the sounds of the computer and the microphone and sends the output to the speakers. A 4-channel mixer can handle up to four different inputs.

Here is a basic setup shown with my real equipment. The standard Lenovo laptop routes to a Peavey 200-watt multichannel mixer. Two cables go from the mixer to two 100-watt Peavey speakers. You could add a microphone from the mixer (and have on its own separate volume channel).

Ancillary Stuff

The speakers, mixer and computer form the central devices needed to crank out high-quality sound to the masses. However, there are some other things that are necessary to complete the package.

As mentioned before, a microphone and microphone stand are absolute necessities. You can buy a microphone stand for under $50 at any music store or even an electronics store. Buy a sturdy, strong microphone stand that you can assemble yourself. When you are not using it, you should be able to store it away so it doesn't get broken.

Buy two high-quality microphones, even though you will only be using one. It is important to have a backup. When the microphone decides to not work (and it will happen), you can have a dependable backup that is only arms-length away. Buy a high-quality microphone— I learned this the hard way. After I first bought the speakers and amplifier, I purchased the cheapest microphone I could find. All microphones are the same, right? That's what I figured, and I was completely wrong. I found out at the most inopportune time.

We were DJing a wedding, and the bride and groom were quite popular people, as evidenced by a constant stream of people making their way to the stage to speak their praises to the happy couple. However, it was at that moment that my $20 cheap microphone decide it was going to stop working. It would work, but only if you held the microphone at a particular angle. So I sat there, stressed and frustrated, as family members and friends tried to tell the bride and groom how wonderful they were, hoping that the microphone would not cut out. Every time someone tipped the microphone a few degrees higher or lower, their voices were completely cut out.

People who come up to use your microphone aren't going to hold it gently and tenderly. They are going to probably be half-drunk anyway, and if they can make their way up to the stage without falling down, they are going to grip that microphone and start slurring into it with force. Make sure to go to a music store and buy a microphone that you would use if you were in a heavy-metal band. Tell the music store sales person that you are going to be swinging the microphone around and dropping it all over the place. Then buy two of them, just to be safe—and keep your backup microphone with your equipment for the inevitable day when your microphone has had enough and decides to quit.

The other piece of ancillary equipment are cables. You will need cables from your computer to your mixer, and from your mixer to the speakers. Make sure that they are long enough! Most cables that come with the speakers are about 4 to 8 feet. This might be long enough, but you should grab two 16-foot cables just to be safe. For a few extra dollars, you will save yourself a ton of stress. The tips of the cables should be designed for mono, not stereo sound.

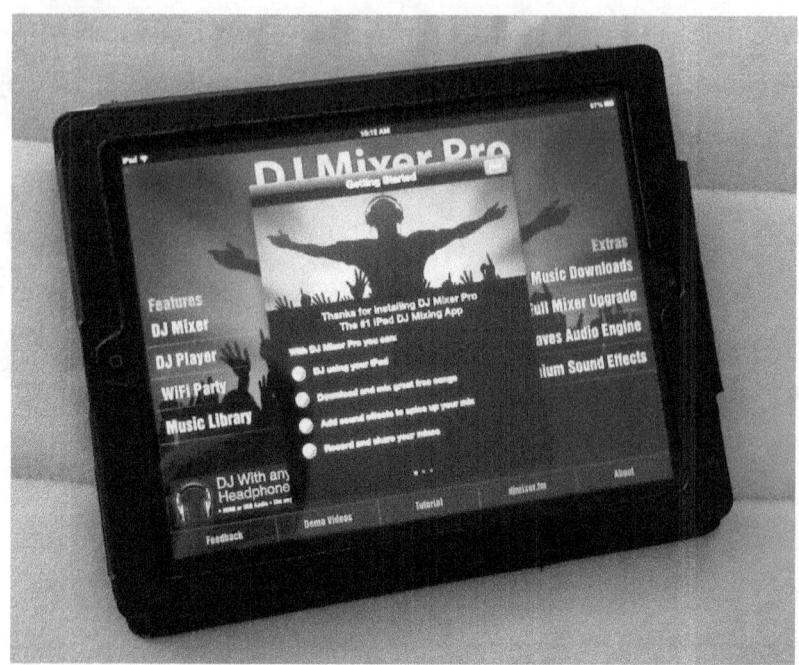

You don't have to use a laptop to play and mix music. My iPad is running DJ Mixer Pro, one of many free & low-cost apps acquired through iTunes.

Mono vs. Stereo Sound

You've probably heard that stereo sound is the greatest, since commercials and radio stations all advertise "in rich, stereo sound". What's the difference between mono and stereo?

Imagine listening to a Beatles' CD on your headphones. If it is in stereo, you will hear vocals coming out of one side, a violin coming out of the other—in other words, you are listening to two separate feeds of music (one for each ear). If you have two speakers, and the music is broadcast in stereo, that means that certain music is coming out of one speaker, and other music is coming out of the other speaker. What happens if the speakers are twenty feet apart, at either side of a stage at a community hall? Someone on the west side of the building will hear vocals and bass, and people at the other side of the building might hear only drums and guitar. You want to make sure that you are using mono. Mono means that both the left and the right speakers crank out exactly the same sound—it is as if you have two "single" speakers.

For DJing, I recommend mono sound. This is because you will have the speakers at different sides of the stage, and some people will be on the dance floor (in the middle of the two speakers), while others are near the back of the room, and still others are off to the sides at the buffet or even outside having a cigarette. The point is, no matter where they are, they shouldn't be hearing half a song, which is what would happen if you were playing your music in stereo and they were standing off to one side. Even if they were near the middle, one side of the song (one speaker) would be louder and more prominent than the other. Stereo sound is great if you are listening to headphones, or in a room with speakers at home. This is because the speakers (or headphones) in your living room are very close to the same strength, and they are very close together. They might be a few yards away at most. However, when you are DJing, stereo sound just won't work very well. When you are DJing, you want a clean, consistent sound in a noisy, dark community hall. Simple is better in this case.

To get mono sound, go to a Radio Shack or electronics store and find a tip for the audio cables that are "stereo / mono" converters. This tip will snap on to the end of the cable coming out of the computer and change any stereo sound into the mono sound that you want. You might even have a setting in the computer that you enable you to play in mono sound, depending on the type of sound card that you have inside your computer.

Other Stuff

Don't forget to include extra supplies when you travel—an extra microphone, a couple of rolls of packing or duct tape, some pens, some paper and at least two good-quality extension cords. Think about a water bottle and a small bottle of aspirin or Tylenol. Consider bringing a small lamp, extra business cards, and even a second change of clothes. You just never know if you will be overdressed, underdressed, or fall in a mud puddle while running off to the bathroom—anything can and will happen if you DJ long enough!

DJing In The Club: Remixing, Beat Matching and Beat Mixing

When I tell people that I DJ, a common response is for someone to start talking like a gangsta and pretend to scratch a record. The truth is, whether you are using turntables, a computer, or CD players, you need to master the hardware and use it to your advantage.

Clubs and bars will often have their own DJ booth with their own equipment. Still, it's a good idea to bring your own. However you decide to do it, beat mixing is a crucial skill to learn and master if you want to be an elite club DJ.

Beat mixing has been around for almost half a century, when DJs began fading one song into another with the intention of having no dead air in-between songs. However, this can prove difficult, as many songs don't have the same tempo or beat. Therefore, the DJ's job is to cross from one song into another seamlessly. Often DJs will have headphones on that allow them to hear music independent of what is actually playing to the audience through the speakers.

Beat matching and beat mixing are basic techniques in the electronic and dance music genres. It is standard for clubs to have non-stop music all night, regardless of the number, type or differences in the songs that are being played.

An example of a remix would be to take a song that is popular on the radio, and either take a sample guitar riff, the chorus or another snippet, and then rework it into a different sounding arrangement. The familiar sounds and the unique arrangement are the key. It must be similar enough that people "get it"—that is, they understand which song you are working. However, as a club DJ, you may have the freedom to basically create your own work of art from other artists' music.

Today's club DJs use several turntables and / or CD players along with a mixer to blend pre-recorded sounds while maintaining a constant beat.

The beat mixing technique consists of the following steps:

- While the song is playing, beat match a new record to it, using headphones for monitoring. Use gain (or trim) control on the mixer to match the levels of the two different songs.

- Restart the new record at the right time. (This is called a slip-cue).

- Before fading in the new track, check that the beats of two tracks match by listening to both channels together in the headphones, as the sound from the speakers can reach you with a delay.

- Gradually fade in parts of the new track while fading out the old track. While in the mix, ensure that the tracks are still synchronized, adjusting the tempo and volume if needed.

It's important to note that the pitch and tempo of a track are normally intertwined. If you spin a disc 10 per cent faster, this means that you are increasing the tempo by 10%. Thus, the pitch will also be 10 per cent higher. This could sound a little strange—remember the Chipmunks albums? Check out DJ software that can change pitch and tempo independently using time-stretching and pitch-shifting, allowing harmonic mixing.

BPM means beats per minute, and it is the backbone of the beat mix process. When you play a song, you must count the beats in a minute to see how fast the song really is. For example, if you play a song, use a stopwatch and time one minute. If the song is in 4/4 time (which is standard for most rock and pop tracks), count the beat of the song. Make a note of how fast the song is. For example, if the BPM count is 100, then you would probably want to group that song in which other "100" BPM songs (or ones that are close in speed).

If this sounds like a lot of work, use a computer. Some computer programs are designed to count the beats per minute automatically. Again, the best way to learn about beat mixing is to grab five or six songs and just give it a try in the comfort of your own house. Be creative and don't be afraid to mess up in the privacy of your own room!

As you listen to the song being played on the dance floor, you should cue the next song that you want to match. You can check it out using your headphones, so that only you will hear it. Most songs have an introduction, and these may be a "soft" or a "hard" opening. Similarly, many songs have what could be called an "outro", which is the ending of the song. You will want to match the "outro" of the first song with the "intro" of the second song, and so on. The important part is to start the second song on the same beat as the first song. Then you adjust the volume (decreasing the first song and increasing the second song) so that the first song fades away and is immediately replaced by the second song. This is called "cross fading". Many DJ mixers have a cross fader, which is one switch that automatically decreasing the one song's volume while increasing the next song's volume at the same time. Higher-end computer programs can match the beats automatically.

Generally, try to beat mix songs that are as close together in count as possible. Strive to beat match songs that are about 3 beats apart (so a song that is 100 BPM could be successfully beat matched with a song that is 97 to 103 BPM).

Many DJs also try to increase the BPM during their set, gradually moving from the slower songs to the faster songs. Like a good novel or movie, your song selection gets more exciting and energetic and then concludes.

Chapter 6:
The Music

After buying a computer, setting up speakers, tweaking the mixer settings, and fiddling around with microphones, setting up your business, printing your business cards and creating cute little packets of candy for your clients, you finally get to the fun part—the music!

Let's face it: it's all about the music. Without a great selection of songs, you just won't be a successful DJ, no matter how impressive your hardware and computer programs are. So, where to begin?

It doesn't matter if you are planning on playing classical music, pop and rock, or hip-hop and R&B. The bottom line is that you must put the customer first.

Remember the all-important rule concerning music: *play what the customer wants*.

This "rule" of course has some provisions attached to it. You should not, for example, play ballads all night because one loud married couple continuously demands lovey-dovey songs, while the rest of the audience patiently waits to get going on the dance floor. Sometimes the client (the people getting married, the president of the social club, the mayor) will have a very specific idea of what songs they want—but what about all of the other guests? Aren't they allowed to request songs as well?

You are going to get conflicting requests, especially at weddings, where the client base is very wide-ranging. At most weddings you have little children, teenagers, adults, and senior citizens—all with different tastes in music. How do you please them all?

The short answer is you probably can't—but you can certainly try. The easiest way to deal with a wide variety of clients is to announce at the gig, through your high-end microphone, that you are happy to take requests. This means that people can come up to you at your DJ station and browse through a catalogue. Don't just ask people what they want to hear. I've been to parties where the DJ has nothing written down, and people have gone up to him and asked "can I make a request?" and the DJ says "sure", and then the conversation ends. Unless the customer knows the exact name of the song and the artist, it's all over for the customer. Why not make it easy for the guest at the party? From their point of view, the DJ booth should be a welcoming place where they can get excited about having a great song played, not some intimidating booth where a DJ, with nothing written down, makes it difficult for partygoers to listen to their favorite tunes.

Have something in writing (like a booklet or catalogue) that people can look through. 95% of people at the gig won't know what the names of songs are called, or who sings them. With a catalogue, they can look through and decide what would be fun.

I like to make charts of hot songs and put them right at the front of the catalogue. "Top Chart Busters", "Hot Disco", "Romantic Ballads" and the like provide a quick and easy reference for most people. For example, you can play Boney M's "Rasputin" at every single DJ gig you ever have and it will most likely be met with people running up on the dance floor. That one is a no-brainer. I put that song on my list of "hot retro" titles and then when someone wants to hear an older dance song, it is right there staring them in the face. Sure, you could play it and it would be successful, but if the customer requests it, and then you play it, you have a slam-dunk out there and the customer feels more involved, as if they somehow helped make the evening great. It's win-win when you prominently display your best songs for customers to request.

Put your best songs on the chart. By "best songs", I mean songs that you have played that will get a lot of people up on the dance floor. These are your proven winners. Here are some samples of some "can't miss" songs for different genres:

<u>Retro Rock n' Roll:</u> make sure to play songs that everybody knows and can sing along to. It doesn't matter if the song is incredibly cheesy and that everyone will laugh when you play it—it is a guilty laugh that says "yes, I love this song!".

Rasputin	Boney M
The Twist	Chubby Checker
Footloose	Kenny Loggins
Dancing Queen	ABBA
You Spin Me Round (Like A Record)	Dead Or Alive
Get Down Tonight	KC & The Sunshine Band
Wild Thing	The Troggs
My Sharona	The Knack
Billie Jean	Michael Jackson
Back in Black	AC / DC
Old Time Rock n' Roll	Bob Seger

Sweet Caroline	Neil Diamond
Crazy Train	Ozzy Osbourne
Pretty Woman	Roy Orbison
I Love Rock n' Roll	Joan Jett
Suicide Blonde	INXS
Girls Just Wanna Have Fun	Cyndi Lauper
Everybody Have Fun Tonight	Wang Chung
Celebration	Kool & The Gang
The Safety Dance	Men Without Hats

Romantic Songs: These songs should be sprinkled in for every five or six "fast songs". There is a whole segment of people (mostly men) who simply will not dance to fast songs. You will see them sitting at the table next to the wife or girlfriend who is tugging on his macho arm. If you play a slow song, he can finally get up there and dance with some dignity.

Can You Feel The Love Tonight	Elton John
I Don't Want To Miss A Thing	Aerosmith
Everything I Do (I Do It For You)	Bryan Adams
My Heart Will Go On	Celine Dion
Insensitive	Jann Arden
Can't Help Falling In Love	Elvis Presley
Jeff Healey	Angel Eyes
Just The Way You Are	Billy Joel
November Rain	Guns N Roses
I've Had The Time Of My Life	Bill Medley & Jennifer Warnes

Total Eclipse Of The Heart	Bonnie Tyler
Candle In The Wind	Elton John
Annie's Song	John Denver
Crazy For You	Madonna
Love Hurts	Nazareth
It Must Have Been Love	Roxette
Your Song	Elton John
Wedding Song	James Ingram & John Tesh
Time of My Life (Good Riddance)	Green Day
I Want It That Way	Backstreet Boys

Note the huge variety in these songs (Backstreet Boys, Madonna, Green Day, Elton John). There are hundreds of great ballads out there, and you should know which ones work for you. Another great tool to get people on the dance floor is to play current ballads that are in movies or on the radio. Stay current and the crowd usually reacts positively.

Oldies: These are songs that mostly people forty and over will like, although it is surprising sometimes to see teenagers dancing to Elvis or The Everly Brothers. That is one of the great things about music; you never know who likes what. I once had a group of fifty-something ladies come up to me at a Christmas party and ask to make a request. I handed them the catalogue, but they had already decided: lots of Van Halen! I was a little surprised, but once "Panama" and " Poundcake" hit the airwaves these women were rocking over at the corner table.

In another situation, I was at a corporate New Year's party and the classic Journey song "Don't Stop Believin'" came on. As soon as the power piano started, I was surprised to see one young man in his early twenties bolt to the centre of the dance floor. He not only loved the song, but he knew every word! Was he even born when Journey released that song? You just never know!

Oldies are great to play at a wedding or community party early in the evening as they will satisfy older people who probably will want to leave before the end of the evening. Senior citizens often call it a night around 10 or 11 pm, so you can often save the heavier stuff until later on. Play the oldies early and often. Here are some stellar oldies:

The Twist	Chubby Checker
Can't Help Falling In Love	Elvis Presley
La Bamba	Ritchie Valens
Jumpin' Jack Flash	Rolling Stones
Good Vibrations	Beach Boys
Jailhouse Rock	Elvis Presley
Old Time Rock n' Roll	Bob Seger
Bye Bye Love	Everly Brothers
Tequila	The Champs
Wild Thing	The Troggs
Bad Bad Leroy Brown	Jim Croce
Let's Twist Again	Chubby Checker
I Feel Good	James Brown
I Got You Babe	Sonny & Cher
Joy To The World	Three Dog Night
She Loves You	The Beatles
Earth Angel	Penguins
The Great Pretender	The Platters
I'm A Believer	Monkees

I Wanna Hold Your Hand	The Beatles

It is worth mentioning that many of these songs are absolutely "can't miss" on the dance floor, but you'll virtually never hear them on many radio stations. One example is the Chubby Checker songs "The Twist" and "Let's Twist Again". These are classics and almost everyone over forty knows them. Yet they aren't usually on the radio to any great extent. There are certain "classics" that every dance could have, and Chubby Checker is definitely a staple of the wedding circuit. Don't be embarrassed to play "cheesy" pop tunes; these are almost always what the customers want to hear.

What are cheesy songs? A great example of this sort of thing is the song "Achy Breaky Heart" by Billy Ray Cyrus. No one in their right mind will admit to owning this CD, although he sold millions of copies in the 1990s. If you play "Achy Breaky Heart" at the right gig, chances are good that many ladies will groan... and then promptly grab their husband, loved one, or some poor unsuspecting guy sitting alone at a table, laugh, and get up on the dance floor.

Country & Regional Music: Depending on where you live, you may find a large demand for other types of music, such as country or Maritime music. Examples of this include Shania Twain and George Strait being hugely popular in western cities like Calgary, Alberta and southern United States, while Great Big Sea is huge out in eastern Canada. Bruce Springsteen and Bon Jovi are huge in New Jersey, since this is the area that they are from. Check your local pubs to see if there are different kinds of music being played. For example, an Irish pub would play a much different variety of music than a country bar, and both would be very different than a sports bar.

<u>Holiday Songs:</u> Some of the most fun gigs that you can DJ are
Halloween parties. Usually the crowd is dressed up in wild costumes,
the atmosphere is fun and the dance hall is filled with spooky decorations
like spider webs and pumpkins.

Make sure to play "Halloween" songs like Michael Jackson's
"Thriller" and anything with a reference to hell, such as AC/DC's
"Highway to Hell" and "Hell's Bells". Warren Zevon came out with a
smash hit "Werewolves of London" and it is usually a classic-rock staple
around Halloween. Be sure to decorate your DJ booth as well!

For Christmas parties, make sure to grab a Christmas compilation
CD at the music store. Often bands or singers will come out with
Christmas albums—Mariah Carey and Boney M have two very popular
Christmas albums, for example. John Mellencamp did a very successful
version of "I Saw Mommy Kissing Santa Claus" and Bruce Springsteen
did a cover of "Santa Claus Is Coming To Town". Scan through the
holiday section and see what popular artists are pumping out for the
Christmas season.

For New Year's Eve, make sure to have "Auld Ang Syne" on hand
for when the clock strikes midnight. Follow that up with U2's "New
Year's Day" and everyone on the dance floor will think you are a genius.

Specialty Music

One of the best parts of the party for a lot of people are prizes—hey, everyone likes free stuff! Door prizes, raffle tickets, 50/50 draws... there are usually prizes or contests of some sort at almost any party. At weddings, for example, there is a bouquet toss, and at company functions there are usually raffle draws or door prizes. Make sure that you have "specialty" music on hand that you can play when the time is right. You can usually find TV and movie theme songs, special effects, or short comedic jingles that will really bring life to the party. Examples of this include:

Is there a game where there is guessing or trivia involved? Play the theme music to the game shows "Jeopardy" or "The Price Is Right" in the background.

Is there a person giving a humorous monologue? If he says something that embarrasses a co-worker, play a 'sad trumpet' sound or a low-pitched foghorn.

If there is any trash-talking or pumping up the crowd for an upcoming event (such as a company function where teams are competing against other) you could play the them to the movie Rocky ("Gonna Fly Now").

There are humorous examples of noises (a burp, a bouncing ball, a screeching car brakes, and the list goes on and on) that you could play in the event of a speech, contest or other "funny" moments during the night.

Finding Popular Music

It's important to stay current if you want to be a popular DJ, regardless of what your specialty is. Many people want to hear the latest great tracks. There are many different ways to expand your music knowledge and find out what is popular. It should be noted that no one will know all the latest songs. However, if you want this to be your specialty, make sure that it matches the type of gigs that you will playing. For example, if you are working high school proms, you definitely need current, hip music. However, if you are playing a family-friendly county fair, you definitely will want to have some "oldies" in there that most everyone will have heard of.

Check out your local arenas and see who has played in your city in the past few years. (The larger arenas will often have websites that have "event calendars" that show who is coming up, and who has played there in the past). You can also check out Ticketmaster's website (www.ticketmaster.ca or www.ticketmaster.com) to see who is coming to your town in the near future.

Another great way you can find out what is popular is to check out www.billboard.com. Billboard is a music industry magazine that has different charts for different types of music. They feature the top 100 singles, top albums, and different genres of music.

Different TV stations usually have their own websites as well, and these websites contain charts, or listings of popular music. The biggest music stations in Canada are MuchMusic, MuchMoreMusic and Country Music Television. In the United States, there are lots of music channels like VH1 and MTV. Recently MTV Canada has launched, and although it doesn't have as many music videos as the other stations, they do offer band interviews and up-to-date trends that appeal to young people and teenagers. Each of these TV stations have their own website—they feature current hits and lots of music content. Of course, in the United States, there are local radio stations, local television stations and endless music stations on the internet.

Another great and easy way to get the best tracks of the year is to buy "best of" compilation CDs. Examples of these include the *MuchDance* series, the *NOW* series of CDs, and *Country Heat*. There are many other "best of" series and they are usually available at your local music store or online. These CDs have one or two tracks by an artist, and they are usually their biggest singles. It's a great way to amass a large collection of hits without breaking the bank and buying 400 different albums. Just go into your local music store and browse around. Compilation discs are very popular and you should be able to find many, many options.

This is especially helpful if you are not knowledgeable about a certain genre of music. For example, I am not particularly well versed in country music, as it's not a type of music that I particularly enjoy. So I buy the "Best Of" country once a year and that gives me big hits if I ever need them. You can look like a truly tapped-in professional by playing a couple hits and no one needs to know that you don't know or care for that genre of music.

Of course, don't forget about co-workers, friends and family. Just tell them that you are on the hunt for great new songs, and you might be surprised at how much advice you receive. Many people enjoy telling their friends about the latest hot tracks, just like people enjoy discussing movies or TV shows. Make sure to ask questions and listen to what they are listening to and enjoying. If you are over at someone's house for dinner or drinks, make sure to ask them to play their favorite CDs and see what comes up!

Music Services

Some DJs use professional music services to supply their music. Instead of traveling to the music store and purchasing CDs, these services just send you mix CDs of the singles that are the big hits in your area. These services usually cost a few hundred dollars a year. Many radio stations also use this type of service, as they can acquire the singles and not have to worry about the other songs on the album, also known as "filler".

These companies come and go, so the best thing to do in this case is just google "DJ music suppliers".

These types of services can be really useful for the DJ who needs to stay current. For most weddings, you probably won't need the hottest new dance tracks. The service can be rather expensive, especially if you subscribe to more than one. However, it is definitely a great way to increase your music library quickly. The benefits of this is that the company does the research and delivers your music right to you door. The recordings are the highest standard and it is 100% legal to use.

Fun Songs

Every wedding has certain "fun songs", or songs that the DJ plays that involves dancing a certain way. Here are some examples of songs that don't fit under "popular" music, but people will request them anyway. Have them on hand and look like a hero.

The Chicken Dance: You can find this on mix CDs for children, or wedding compilation CDs. When this song comes on, eighty-year-olds grab their eight-year-old grandkids and run up to the dance floor with big smiles on their faces. People will flap their arms like chickens, strut around and generally act crazy.

The Macerena: This song was hugely popular in the 1990s and is performed by the band Los Del Mar. Mostly women will dance to this one—they usually get in a big line and then do slow-motion aerobics for a few minutes.

Rasputin: This one is my all-time favorite DJ song. It always gets people out on the dance floor. The highlight is halfway through the song when people usually get in a circle, start clapping, and a few bold people begin dancing in "Russian" style, folding their arms and kicking out their legs. It's hilarious and loads of fun. The very popular band Boney M recorded this song and it has remained a staple for years.

Waltzes: Make sure that you have some old 1950s waltzes on hand. Invariably at a wedding, you will get requests some senior citizens for some big band or swing music, or classic waltzes. You can just grab a "best of" waltz CD at your local music store and have it ready just in case.

Line Dances: Depending on the party, you might get requests to line dance songs. These would include Billy Ray Cyrus' "Achy Breaky Heart" or the Nitty Gritty Dirt Band, who put out two great line dance songs: "Fishin' In The Dark" and "Cadillac Ranch". Any songs that get a large number of people up on the dance floor is always a good thing.

Games: If your client wants to play a game during the wedding reception or birthday party, make sure that you know about it in advance.

Ask them if they have any special requests for songs. If so, make sure to have some fun songs that work for "musical chairs" or similar style games. Popular, upbeat songs include *Funky Cold Medina* by Tone Loc, *The Loco-Motion* (covered by a number of bands), *Dancing Queen* by ABBA, etc. Make sure that the song is upbeat and popular—the more people who know the song, the better.

Radio Songs Versus Remixes

As a general rule for corporate parties or family events (such as weddings): *play the radio version (single version) of the song.* You might hear a song on the radio and buy their single at the local music store. Often, the band will put remixes on the CD single. These are different versions of the same song. For example, the drums might be remixed differently, or the vocals extended, or it might be a "dance remix" with a loud, bass-thumping dance groove. These are great tracks—under the right circumstances. Remember, most people at a dance won't be huge fans of any one band. This means that they aren't going to appreciate a remix of a popular single. Most of the times, they are just going to want to hear the radio version of the single, because it is the one version that they know. Watching people dance to a song that they think they know, but don't, can be painful. People want to dance to songs that they know and can sing along with.

As the DJ, you might get the urge to play obscure tracks because they are "awesome". Don't do it. Stick to popular songs that most of the audience will know. You might think that a hot dance track that you heard at the local club is great, but you might only have ten other people in the dance hall love the track, while the other two hundred yawn and go sit down. Take a look at the audience and see what they are dancing to.

The goal is to keep as many people up on the dance floor as possible while at the same time providing a mix of different types of music.

Of course, if you are playing a cutting-edge dance, or you are in the club, then by all means remix it up! People will go to these types of events to hear the latest, hottest fresh mixes—if you played a vanilla radio song they would probably boo you off of the stage! Make sure you know your audience and be attentive—you can afford to throw in a loser once in a while, but eventually you should be knocking them out of the park with every song.

The Song Deconstructed

Considering how many thousands upon thousands of pop songs have been recorded, it is amazing that the general structure of a single remains largely unchanged over the past 50 years. Here's a breakdown of how a basic song is manufactured. This applies mainly to pop songs and radio songs. Of course, there are exceptions to the rules (Pink Floyd albums immediately come to mind), but here I am referring to the average single that you would hear on a pop, country or rock radio station.

- The Intro: the song either has a "hard" opening or a "soft" opening. Hard openings are introductions that begin right away. Examples of a hard opening would be the Beatles "Hey Jude", U2's "Mysterious Ways", and the Red Hot Chili Peppers' "Give It Away". These songs begin with a hard beat and have no fade in or soft instrumental. A soft intro can be thought of as the opposite of a fade out. Examples of a soft opening are the Bee Gee's "Jive Talkin", Metallica's "Enter Sandman" and the Hollies "Long Cool Woman

(In A Black Dress). These songs don't start right away; they have a longer opening before getting into the meat of the song.

- The Post: Have you ever noticed that the radio DJ will talk over the opening of a song? They will discuss the weather, the upcoming concert, or just blab endlessly right until the lead singer starts actually singing? This part of the song, where the vocals begin, is called the post. If you are mixing or beat matching from one song to the next, you want to be done your fade-in and fade-out by this point.

- Verse 1: This is the first verse / vocal segment. It is usually the most identifiable part of the song. If you are remixing, you want to leave this part of the song alone so that most people will identify it.

- The Chorus: This is also known as the hook. The chorus is often repeated throughout the song and is usually somehow related to the song's title. For example, "She moves in mysterious ways, it's alright, it's alright, it's all-right," is the chorus for the song that is aptly named "Mysterious Ways" by U2.

- Verse 2: This verse is structured the same as the first verse, although the lyrics will almost always be different.

- The Chorus: This is repeated and will sound nearly identical to the first chorus.

- Solo: Different styles of music will have different solos. In heavy metal, for example, the solo is a whining, fast-moving guitar. In a ballad, it might be a piano or string arrangement. It might even just be a chorus or a verse that is played without vocals.

- Verse 3: There is usually one more verse after the solo, and it is sometimes abridged before heading into the final chorus.

- The Chorus: This is the final chorus of the song.

- <u>The Ending:</u> Also known as the "outro", the ending of the song can be "hard" or "soft" similar to the intro. This is generally where the club DJ will mix out of the song and match it up to the next song's intro.

Knowing the song structure will help you to mix songs from one to another, and it may also be useful if you decide to end a song early. It is important to know how your songs begin and end. You would not normally mix a soft outro with a hard intro, because the song would slowly fade out... only to be replaced by a quick intro that would disrupt the flow of the music. Generally speaking, you should try to match soft outros of the first song with soft intros of the second song so that they seem to flow right into each other.

If you disagree with the above statement... then great! There are no hard and fast rules. Try it for yourself and see what you like and don't like. Sometimes it helps to bounce ideas off of friends and ask them what they think.

Handling Conflicting Requests

A number of years ago, while DJing a community hall party, I received a number of requests for country music. We had played the hall a couple of months earlier, in the middle of the sweltering, hot summer, for a Stampede party and played non-stop country music for six hours straight. I recognized many of the same members of the community at this dance as well, although we were now in the autumn and things were considerably cooler. I wanted to make sure that I wasn't just playing the same songs from the Stampede party. The same couple continued to come up to us and repeatedly asked for "more country!". I acquiesced and played quite a few country songs.

I then talked to a couple of other people who came up and asked us why we were playing so much country. We asked if they had any requests and they opined "anything but country!".

You will no doubt receive very vague "requests" while DJing. I have received countless requests from people for "something fun". Of course, that means something completely different to almost every single person. What is a "romantic" song, for example? Is a new R&B song romantic? An old Beatles song? What about a George Michael ballad? Elton John? An instrumental? Everyone would have their own special romantic songs, and no one would entirely agree with each other on what they are.

If you receive vague requests, point them to the catalogue and do your best. Don't sweat it if people have no idea what they want to hear. Most of the time, people will request really obscure tracks that most people have never heard of. Offer a more "radio friendly" alternative if you don't have the track. If you do have it, however, play it. One trick that we use is to try to "make them a deal". We usually say something like, "hey, we'll play it, but you have to make sure to get up there dance to it!". Most of the time they will do exactly that. There's nothing worse than playing a requested song and watching the dance floor clear. The party goers all sit in their chairs and wonder why the DJ lost his mind and is playing this obscure loser track. Often I've wanted to grab the microphone in the middle of the track and yell "it wasn't me! It was that guy! He made me play it!" Have a sense of humor and don't sweat it if you play a dog once in a while. Recover by going to your "heavy hitters"—those songs that you have on hand that will get lots of people back up on the dance floor. It is like you are the coach and your songs are your athletes. Make sure to have your top line sitting there waiting, and when you are in trouble, call up your stars and let them score!

Mixing It Up

What is the proper mix of ballads to rock songs? Dance songs to oldies? If the answer were so simple that I could write it down, everyone could DJ. In fact, if it were that easy, people could just buy a "mix CD" and pop it in their CD player and never use your services!

But of course, DJing is more than just playing tracks like a mix CD. It's also about taking requests and feeling the room for the right songs. Usually, at a wedding or community hall party, you should play two or three songs of the same genre. You are going to find that there will be a group of people who love country songs. Then there will be a group of people who enjoy oldies. Some people will only dance to ballads, and still others will dance to 80s music or pop songs only.

Don't just play one song from each genre. Often at a party, it takes up to two minutes to people to put down their drink, find their spouse or friend, and make it up to the dance floor. If you play a classic ballad, like a slow Eagles song or an Elton John track, follow it up with a similar song as chances are the same group of people will want to dance to the second song.

Here's an example of a play list that might not work:

- Elton John: Can You Feel The Love Tonight
- Guns N Roses: Paradise City
- Shania Twain: Don't Be Stupid
- Bee Gees: Stayin' Alive
- Celine Dion: My Heart Will Go On

By the time that you get the "Elton John" crowd up on the dance floor, the track will be half over. When you start playing the next track, a fast Guns N Roses track, a significant portion of the crowd might leave. By the time the "Guns N Roses" crowd gets up on the dance floor, the track is half over, and then a country track comes on. Eyes will roll and the heavy-metal people will leave while the country people shuffle up onto the dance floor. And so on, until people just sit in their chairs and wonder when the DJ is going to "play something good".

Alternatively, here's a play list that will make people get up and dance:

- Boney M: Rasputin
- Bee Gees: Stayin' Alive
- Dead Or Alive: You Spin Me Round
- Aerosmith: I Don't Want To Miss A Thing
- Faith Hill: Breathe
- Shania Twain: Don't Be Stupid

Note that some of the songs are the same, but the order has been moved around and the songs flow into each other. When the retro dance people hear Boney M, they will get up and dance. But they will also stay up for the Bee Gees and Dead Or Alive. These are all fast retro dance songs. The "bridge" song, or the song that bridges different genres, is a ballad but also a retro band, Aerosmith. But the song is a newer release from the band, so people who don't like retro music will also get up and dance. Plus it's a ballad, so that means that many new people will get up and dance.

The "ballad people" will stay up on the floor for Faith Hill. But the "country people" will also want to get up and dance. Since it takes about half a song to get up on the dance floor, the country people will be ready to dance when a fast country song comes on (The Shania Twain track).

If you "pair up" your dance songs and have "bridge songs", you will keep many more people up on the dance floor. This way, you can have a great variety of music and satisfy the whole party. This might become instinctual after a while, but it can also be a good idea to write down some song sets that you think will work in advance. Try grouping six or seven songs together and then try them. If they work, great! If not, go back to the drawing board and see what else you can try. Make sure to write down what works after your set as well. If you were happily surprised by a mix of three or four songs, write it down and note it for a future gig.

When you flip from one song to the next, that is called "segueing". When one song gets quieter and the next song gets louder, that is called "cross fading". The most important thing to remember when bring up song 2 and dissolving song 1 is to keep your hand on the master volume. Songs tend to be recorded at different volumes, and it's important to have a seamless segue from one song into the next. All sorts of things can go wrong during a DJ event, but one of the most disastrous is when the music is too loud—especially if this happens suddenly. With the size and power of professional DJ speakers, the wrong volume can be annoying and downright painful for your audience.

Don't let the first song fade out completely before bringing in the second song. The whole idea of cross fading is to keep the energy level up, so when song 1 is fading out, begin bringing in song 2. There is no hard-and-fast rule for this, but usually the last ten seconds of a song, if it's fading out, can be faded out pretty quickly. The key here is to practice keeping that energy level up.

Do not let the two mixed songs transition for very long—usually ten seconds is plenty, with only about three or four seconds of volume that is loud enough that people will hear both songs. Quickly fade from one to the other.

In The Clubs

Club DJing is totally different than corporate DJing. At corporate gigs, you are basically playing radio-friendly dance music that might get progressively more aggressive as the night goes on. At the club, however, your job is to get that dance floor packed and get as loud and raucous as possible.

Things occur at the clubs that would make corporate party planners' hair turn grey. It is very important to differentiate one type of gig from another. At the clubs, you will want to supply big sound, heavy bass, and lots of beat-mixing. This means that you will want to merge one track into another and keep the beats somewhat the same; by doing this, you are ensuring that the dance floor is one long dance marathon. Ballads are few and far between, and the more hard-core and current you can get, the better.

Why don't nightclubs and bars just play songs on a CD? Some do, and most have very average results. The simple explanation is that bar owners generally know how to run a bar, not a dance. They are able to purchase or lease a building, advertise, buy cases of alcohol, pay staff, and generally run an business. They are not experts with current dance music. That's where you come in. Besides, who wants to come all the way out to a club to hear a CD? Many people want to hear what specific DJs are going to play—it is fun and exciting!

As a club DJ, you will have freedom to do things that the corporate gigs will not do. For example, you can try out new songs at clubs—this is generally encouraged, because most young people at clubs want to hear the next great track. People at corporate events, however, usually want to dance to songs that they know already.

If you are interested in approaching a club or a bar, make sure to spend a couple of months learning how to beat-mix and merge songs together. Get wild and creative. If it is truly a passion, then the time will fly by and you will be ready to roll in eight to ten weeks. Then approach the bar or club owner and present them with a mix CD with your songs that have been spliced, beat-mixed and merged together. If they are interested, great. If not, you might want to offer your services at a substantial discount (or even free) if you really want to gain some experience.

Make sure to advertise yourself at these clubs. Print up some flyers and post them around town—college or university campuses, supermarkets, the library—wherever you can. Remember, as a club DJ, you are the show! You will be building up a name brand for yourself and the club owner will appreciate the promotion as well. Put where you are playing on the flyer and the owner of the club will be impressed that you are able to draw a crowd.

Different Types Of Music

Do you have to be an expert in every single genre of music? What if you don't like heavy metal or country? What if rap gets on your nerves?

The short answer is that if you are considering DJing as a profession, then chances are very good that you already love music and spend considerable time playing it, reading about it, or otherwise enjoying it.

The club DJ will want to get familiar with all sorts of dance, independent, house music and acid tracks. Mobile DJs who work more corporate events such as weddings, private parties and community events will need to know oldies, 60s, 70s and 80s music, as well as a selection of popular radio and dance tracks.

A successful DJ, just like a successful musician, rock star or rapper, understands music in general, is very knowledgeable about one or two genres, and recreationally enjoys many different types of music.

Audience Participation

You may be called upon to get the crowd involved or even to emcee an event. Make sure that know your role when you sign the agreement with the client. There is nothing worse than showing up to a wedding and finding out that you are expected to play longer, announce prizes and contests, or do something that you were unaware of. It will cause you stress, and just as importantly, it will cause stress to the client because they will be surprised as well. No one likes surprises at an event—you and the client want to know exactly what is going to happen and when. Surprises are almost always bad.

If you are asked to emcee an event, there are a few basic ground rules. The first and most important one is to ask for more money. Being the emcee is a lot of work, and even if you are a natural, it is still a lot of responsibility. Being an emcee means that not only will you be playing music, but you will also be paying attention to when certain things occur during the night, like cutting the wedding cake, announcing that Aunt Mable lost her car keys, and announcing when and where the wedding party will be available for photographs.

Typically, for a wedding, you should be able to add on $100 or $200 for the emceeing duties when you are first starting out. (If you can get more money, of course, go for it—you should always be asking what the market allows and what you can get). If you are uncomfortable with the emcee role, then simply do not offer that service. It's better to just be honest up front and say that you do not emcee events, even if it means that you don't get the gig. Why put yourself through misery for an evening, do a lousy job and disappoint the client? Life is too short. If emceeing is not something that you want to do, then don't do it.

If you do want to do it, and you are good at it, then welcome to the money club. You can make a lot of money by emceeing events, and if you are good at it, then it will be good money for work that you will be skilled at. It is like watching a doctor operate—it may take him fifteen minutes to give you stitches, but he has thousands of hours of schooling and work behind him. It is the same with being an emcee—it may look easy, and if you do enough events, it will become "easy" in that it can be second-nature to run the show. Note however, that you are getting paid well because of the responsibility that you are taking on, not necessarily because of the effort. If you are a naturally good speaker, can listen well, have a pleasant demeanor, can run an event from the podium, and don't mind three hundred strangers watching your every move, then you will probably enjoy being the emcee.

You will have some key responsibilities and duties as emcee. The most important one is to be aware of what your role is. You are not the show. Your job as emcee is to introduce the speakers, the guests of honor, and to keep the evening running on schedule. Let me repeat—you are not the show. If you can make the other speakers look good, then you have done your job.

Don't try to be funny. Remember, you will probably be in a room full of hundreds of strangers. Chances are good that you will not personally know the bride, groom, or anyone else for that matter. Just be professional and keep the evening running on time.

Be prepared. Speakers at an event should give you an introduction in advance. Read it over and make sure that you know how to pronounce any last names, places, or phrases that may not be familiar. This is a big deal—if you mispronounce a name, everyone at the event who knows that person will cringe. If the speaker doesn't bother to give you an introduction that is written down or in advance, try to talk to them before they go on stage and make sure that you can present a little mini-introduction.

It is really important for the emcee to keep the event moving. There have been countless awards shows, banquets, wedding receptions, and corporate parties where the speaker in question (and the emcee, for that matter) talk for way too long. Five minutes is a really long time to listen to someone talk, especially for people wearing formal clothes. The audience is there to be entertained, and that means that whatever you as the emcee can do to keep the show moving, you should do it.

That sometimes means putting up with people who speak. They will drone on for way too long. People love the sound of their own voice. Remember, not everyone who is speaking will be a professional, and as such, they might be more prepared about what they want to say rather than what the audience wants to hear. If possible, establish a time limit (like five minutes) with your clients and then try to stick to it. Tell your speakers that they have five minutes, and then discreetly glance at your watch or the clock on the wall to gage their time left.

This is an ideal situation, and the "five minute" rule just might not be feasible for every event. No one (including you as the emcee) will have the guts to tell the millionaire uncle who sponsored the whole wedding that he is only able to talk for five minutes. In that case, you will pretty much have to let him bore the audience to tears for fifteen minutes while he tells his pointless anecdote to the poor people at the tables. However, you could have an agenda worked out in advance and perhaps you can agree with your client that if things are running long, then certain items or people will get cut. This can be a painful situation at a wedding and just might not be worth it. Besides, sometimes people just expect that weddings (like awards shows on TV) will just run on way too long. However, sometimes there are things that can be spaced out more evenly to inject some life into the festivities, such as following up a speech with a slide slow, and then maybe a relative who is playing an acoustic guitar, and then another speech.

With that being said, you are getting paid regardless of whether these family members are entertaining. Control what you can, do your best and don't sweat the small stuff. No one is going to blame you directly because uncle Albert took half an hour to tell a three-minute story.

Remember, if you are thinking that the speaker is boring, chances are very good that the other hundred audience members are thinking the same thing. Before you start the program, tell the speakers that you will give them a signal when they are halfway through their time allotment, and you will give them another signal when they have one minute left. Make sure to tell them that the time schedule is important for the success of the program. Explain, if necessary, that if they run long, it eats up another speaker's time. Most people will understand that, since they don't want to intrude on a relative's speech. If they get up there and go long, you might have to literally walk up and stand next to them as a physical reminder that they are done. If this doesn't work, you might have to literally interrupt when they stop to take a breath (they will have to eventually) and take the podium back. It may be uncomfortable, but the audience will silently thank you. Sometimes (hopefully), this duty falls to the best man or someone familiar with the family. They get to be the bad guy who everyone is secretly thankful for.

An good emcee will keep the energy in the room and this means being able to handle transitions from one speaker to another. Imagine, for example, at a wedding reception, and uncle Harry tells an amazing story that has the audience crying with laughter. You get up and as the emcee, quickly introduce Grandma Wilma, who proceeds to begin telling a very moving, sad story about a death in the family and a long-suffering family member's losing battle with Alzheimer's disease. When she is done, the best man gets up and immediately tells a hilarious story about the groom, four bottles of tequila and his three nights in a Mexican prison.

These three speakers are all very different, and after each speaker, it will fall on the emcee to bring the audience back to a neutral state of mind before the next speaker. You will be putting the next speaker at a disadvantage if the previous speaker doesn't match the flow of the following speaker. If the speech was very moving or sad, try to follow it up with a quote, a little story, a longer-than-normal introduction for the next guest, or some such transition that will allow the audience to literally get their breath, have a drink of water and refocus on the next presenter.

Remember that a really good emcee is very hard to find. If you are successful at it, you can command a great deal of money in addition to your DJ fee.

Chapter 7:
Teaming Up With A Band

Some people, when they book their wedding, are adamant about having a real band play at their party. Others would rather save some money and have a DJ. Some enjoy both. A great way to get extra business is to join with a local band.

The word "synergy" basically means to create more than the sum of the parts. Business people like to use the word because it means that if everything works together, you get more without actually spending more. The concept is like 1+1=3. If the first "1" is you, and the second "1" is the band, then instead of adding up to 2, which is the amount of business that you would get on your own, the magic number of "3" translates into a higher customer satisfaction rating, a better experience for your clients, and ultimately more business for both the band and you.

So, how do you get the "3"? Better yet, how do you actually find a local band? Finding the right band can be difficult. There are hundreds of bands roaming around out there, but there are very few that you should want to join with. If you are a wedding or corporate DJ, you want to find a band that plays weddings and similar parties. This sort of band should play almost exclusively covers and requests if wedding and community hall parties are your thing. You don't want to find a band that writes and produces their own heavy metal music and then be the DJ in-between their sets with Elton John music!

However, you might want to join forces with the heavy metal band if the gig is right. Maybe they are playing a show at a local pub or bar and you can DJ in between their sets. If that is the case, then you would be working in a "metal" environment and should play similar (but commercially successful) songs, like *Metallica, Guns N' Roses* and newer bands like *Nickelback* or *System Of A Down*. Or, just check with the band. They have some underground acts that want some air time, and they be able to provide you with CDs to use.

Working with a band presents a whole set of opportunities and also a different set of challenges. The following discusses two scenarios: weddings and bars. Both are very different from each other.

The Wedding Team-Up

There are a few ways to find bands that play weddings. The first would be to look online. Sometimes bands have their own websites, and this should give you an idea of the types of music and the types of gigs that they play.

The other way to find bands that play weddings is to ask people who have been married recently and ask them if a band played at their wedding. If so, get their contact info and phone them up or e-mail them.

Another way to locate local bands is to go to events that have "corporate" bands playing. For example, Calgary plays host to the Calgary Exhibition & Stampede every July. For ten days straight, all sorts of malls, community centers and corporations hold Stampede Breakfasts, and many of these events have bands that play cover tunes of popular country songs.

If you work for a company that has a Christmas party, go to it and check out the band if there is one playing at the event. Or, if you have friends who go to Christmas or holiday parties, ask them to grab the band's info (maybe they have a business card or a buddy can get the name and phone number of one of the band members).

Many larger cities have weekly or monthly music magazines or newspapers that showcase local bands. While many of these bands won't fit this particular type of profile, the occasional band might do corporate or cover band gigs and this would be a good fit for weddings. Remember, these are just suggestions to get the blood flowing in your brain—be creative and think of all the different types of paying gigs you could be working.

Once you contact a band and determine that they are a good fit (for example, you hear them play and like their song selection and their style), then ask for the team-up. Basically this means that they will offer your services and you will offer theirs for upcoming gigs. For example, I teamed up with a local band in Calgary called 20 / 20. They have played weddings, parties and all sorts of corporate gigs. They offer "DJ services" on their website, and when someone books a wedding, they ask if they want to purchase additional DJ services for a small fee.

When you are gigging with a band, you will probably make less money than if you DJ the entire event by yourself. Typically, when I team up with a local band, my rate is about half of what I would normally charge. The reason for this is simple: you are using most of the band's gear (speakers, microphone stands, etc.) and the set up time is virtually non-existent for the DJ. You are, in effect, the second banana. In most cases, you will be running your sound through the band's mixer and speakers, and half of the night (or more) will be spent sitting around and listening to the band play. Relative to working by yourself, it's pretty easy money. Besides, you are only working "half a night" since the band is on for as much time as the DJ. Of course, if any of the above scenarios change, such as the DJ being partially responsible for setup, or using some of the DJ's equipment, then the rates should increase accordingly. (If you want to earn more money, ask to be part of the setup crew—hey some roadies make good money!) Being a set up person can be a great opportunity, especially if you are interested in the music business. Learning how to properly set up amplifiers, mixers, drums, guitars and the like can be a really fun and enlightening experience for anyone looking to either start up their own band, work in the music industry, or just be part of the business.

It is important to note, however, that all of these ideas are just guidelines—charge as much money as you can without losing business! After all, the market will determine whether or not your prices are too high. If the price is too high, you will know—no one will book you.

DJing with a band at a wedding or a corporate Christmas party can be a lot of fun. You, along with the band, are providing two different sets of entertainment for the party. As a DJ, you can take requests that the band might not know. A well-rehearsed, veteran band might know fifty or sixty songs (and play them really well), whereas you have over 1,000 songs on hand with the click of a mouse.

Make no mistake about it, however; the band is the headliner and you are the opening act. The DJ will also play in-between the 45-minute sets that most corporate bands will play. A typical night might feature the following itinerary:

8:00 p.m. to 9:00 p.m. – DJ plays classic rock and ballads

9:00 p.m. to 9:45 p.m. – The band plays their first set

9:45 p.m. to 10:15 p.m. – DJ plays mix of dance and rock

10:15 p.m. to 11:00 p.m. – The Band plays second set

11:00 p.m. to 11:30 p.m. – The DJ plays heavy dance mix

11:30 p.m. to end of show – The band plays last set

Note that when the band is playing, you can basically take a half hour off. You can go for a walk, have a drink, or get some fresh air. It can work out really well for both the band and the DJ. When I DJ these sorts of gigs, I will often leave my DJ gear set up so that I can flick a switch and come to the rescue in the event that the band suffers from a technical problem.

It all comes down to the working relationship you have with the band—are they professional, driven, and very good at what they do? They will be thinking the same thing about you.

The Bar Team-Up

In this case, the scenario is entirely different than working a wedding or a community hall event. As a DJ, you will be working with bands who are playing clubs, bars or dance halls. Typically, the band won't be playing lots of corporate covers and ballads, but rather will be showcasing their own music that they wrote and produced. Often the bands will be selling their own albums at these shows and they might feature very avant-garde, really heavy or artsy music.

These gigs can be a lot of fun, especially if you enjoy the type of music that the band is playing. This is because you can play similar styles of music before and in-between their sets. Customers at pubs are usually more open to different types of music—after all, they are probably there to hear a local band or party.

Sometimes a bar or club will have their own sound system. They have the capability to crank out their own tunes. Why would they hire you at all? Often it is because the owner of the club knows that having a professional DJ, with their own equipment and knowledge about songs, will get more thirsty people into his bar. It's all about increasing the business for the bar—remember this when you are trying to get bar gigs. The bar or club might have two or three mix CDs that they play when there's no one around (like on the weekdays), but on Friday night, when the place is full, they want a DJ in the house who can take requests, get on the microphone and get the crowd pumped up, and churn out hit after hit.

Finding a club-level band is relatively easy. Start by checking out the local music papers and seeing if some bands are playing local clubs. Also, go downtown and scan the clubs for upcoming acts—often the bands will put up posters well in advance of them playing the venue.

Again, going online is always a good idea, although many smaller bands won't have sophisticated websites. You might have to dig around to find a "real" band that actually plays bars or clubs.

Another option would be to visit the local taverns and clubs and ask to speak with the manager. Give them your business card and a letter stating who you are, and explain that you would love to DJ the club on the weekend, evening, or whenever they can use you. The manager just might give you a call when they are stuck, and then you will not only be playing and earning money, but helping out a manager when they need you. Getting your foot in the door is often the hardest part of the industry; once you are in, you might find a regular or steady job with a certain bar or club. Be reliable and professional, and you will be off to a great start.

Again, remember that when you team-up with a band, they are the headliners. You are there to open for them, get the crowd fired up, and then let the band do their thing.

Playing bars and clubs might be more your type of venue, but usually the money is not as good as playing a wedding or a corporate gig. Often bars and clubs will pay a very minimal amount to a band, and then often they will add on more money, depending on how many people show up. Sometimes you will find bar owners who don't mind paying for the booze inventory and the staff, but everything else, including you, is not considered a priority. This means that you might work for six hours on a Saturday night and then have to hen peck the owner for your twenty or thirty dollars. However, if you hook up with the right company and / or the right band, working in a bar can be a great (and fun) way to get some experience, meet some people in the industry, and earn some money. Long term, you could aspire to become a headliner. These DJs play their own remixes or style of music and become a local celebrity of sorts, complete with their own fans who will follow the DJ to the local bar to hear him or her spin tunes.

Chapter 8:
Getting An Agent

Once you have your business set up and few weddings, parties or other events under your belt, you may want to seek the services of an agent. Agents work for you and help increase your sales by finding you events that you can DJ. In return, an agent takes a commission from the event fee.

Let's make one thing perfectly clear right off the bat: you might go your whole career and never use an agent. This entire section is completely optional.

Agents are used in many different industries. For example, if you want to buy my house, chances are good that your real estate agent would contact my real estate agent and the two would negotiate a price that we both were happy with. In fact, you can buy a house and never even meet the actual sellers. Everything can be done through an agent.

When it comes time to pay for your house, you might use a mortgage broker, who is an agent who works for you to shop around and find you the best interest rates. Instead of you phoning up every bank and credit agency and doing the research yourself, the agent or broker does this work for you.

Movie stars and book writers often use the services of agents. These people read scripts, contact movie studios, book publishers and television producers, and generally are "in the know" when it comes to getting things done. Having an agent means that you have someone working for you in order to get to your goal.

In this case, your goal is getting more DJ business. An agent can help you by either finding you new events, or setting you up to work multiple events at a permanent location. For example, you may be a DJ who has played weddings and birthday parties. However, your agent may be able to secure DJ events at local hotels, bars and nightclubs. In addition, an agent might know some hotel and ballroom managers, and you may find yourself with regular opportunities at these establishments. If a corporation is having a big event at the hotel, they may just ask the hotel to provide the entertainment. The hotel manager, who has many other job responsibilities, will just contact the agent and say, "get me a DJ who plays current dance songs for this Saturday please!". If that is the case, you may find a recurring job at a hotel.

How much should you pay an agent? Well, some charge a flat rate, or it might be a percentage. Everything is negotiable. Some agents charge 10 per cent of the fee that is paid out, and others charge more. Often, the client will pay the agent, who deducts his fee, and then forwards the balance on to the DJ.

Meeting The Agent

How do you find an agent? There are often some in the phone book (under "entertainment agencies or entertainment services", online, and some even advertise. You can often just give them a phone call or email and ask to set up a short meeting. Come prepared.

Some agencies work in conjunction with local music unions as well. If you contact a local musicians' union or music industry association, you might find agencies that are looking for new clients.

It is important to be professional when meeting with an agent. This means having a business card, references, and a promotional package that you can hand to the agent. You may only get five or ten minutes, so have your promotional package ready to go so that you can drop it off if time is running short. What is in the promotional package? You should have a flyer, or a handout that lists your services, as well as a couple of references from satisfied (or thrilled) clients. If you are working a gig, why not take a few pictures of your setup, especially it your station looks great? If you made a mix CD, throw that in the package as well. Treat your promo package like your music DJ resume.

Reference letters are one of the easiest and most powerful ways to gain legitimacy in the industry. Hopefully, they will result in the agent or a potential client saying to themselves, "Wow! They played the [well-known] hotel and the managers love them! We should hire that DJ company."

If, for example, you play a hotel on New Year's Eve, and the event went really well, you should then ask the client for a reference letter. Wait a couple of weeks, and then send the client a nice thank-you card or a note expressing your gratitude for the event, and that you wish them the best of luck in the new year. Then, ask if they would write you a reference letter.

It doesn't have to be long-winded or wordy. As long as it is from the client, expresses the great job you did, and has a contact name on there (in case the agent, or future clients wish to follow up), then you are all set. The letter should mention one or all of the following:

- You were responsible

- You were easy to deal with, especially when an unanticipated circumstance arose
- You were professional & on time
- You looked good (were dressed appropriately, groomed)
- Your DJ services sounded good (selection of music & quality of sound)

For bands, one way that you can get your sound out to the general public and to an agent is through a demo tape. This would mean recording a few songs onto a CD and then handing them over to an agent. For the DJ, it doesn't quite work that way. You can, however, use music on your website and include a list of song genres that you are comfortable using during a gig.

If all this sounds like the DJ is preparing an extensive list of references, knocking on the door of the agent, begging for five minutes of his time, and then being chased out the door, think again. Remember, the agent works for you. They make money by using their connections in the music business to get you work. Once they realize that you are dependable and low-maintenance, they will want you just like you want them. The more events you can DJ, the more money the agent makes. It is a partnership, and one that can be very profitable if you hook up with the right contacts and dedicate the time and energy to putting on the best show possible for the client.

The first few events that you work may be scrutinized closely by the agent. Put your best foot forward and go that extra mile. The agent must know that you are dependable and that you are stress-free for the event coordinator and the agent.

June 2012

To Whom It May Concern:

I am happy to provide a reference for the Smith DJ Company. We have used them numerous times throughout the year at our establishment, the Unlucky Hobo Pub.

Smith DJ has provided upbeat, current music and has a professional, positive attitude. We often hear compliments from customers about the quality of music and the dance floor is always packed.

I would gladly recommend Smith DJ Services to anyone who is looking for a punctual, well-groomed and entertaining DJ for their event for party.

Regards,

Jack McHiggins

Lucky Boxcar Pub

Example of a reference letter from a satisfied client.

The Life Of An Agent

I was fortunate to hook up with a local band in Calgary called 20/20 who has been playing corporate parties, weddings, tailgate parties and all sorts of different gigs. The bass player, Dan Cezar, has been in the music business for four decades. He is a walking encyclopedia about the music business and the industry in general. It came as no surprise to me to discover that Dan has spent a significant amount of his energy as an agent for other bands when he wasn't playing bass. (For more on 20/20, see the appendix at the back of this book.)

"I started playing when I was twelve or thirteen," Cezar notes. "There will always be better bass players, or guitar players, or great singers out there. It's not always about finding the best, most proficient musicians. Rather, I've found that it is about finding the right pieces to fit together. That is what makes a great band."

Cezar became an agent in the mid-1980s, primarily because he was interested in the business side of the music industry. "I wanted to stay involved in the business, and I taught bass lessons in my spare time," he notes. "I was also booking bands, hotels, conventions, weddings, and parties. There were many times when I got calls to book our band, and we were already booked. So I thought, 'hey, maybe I should be booking other bands and getting involved that way'. I was very well tapped in with about six other agents."

Cezar notes that it is important for bands and DJs to be professional and want to make the client happy. "As an agent, I was going for bands that I wanted and believed in, because the whole idea is to make the client happy with the band. When I say client, I mean the hotel or establishment. This ultimately leads to a position where the hotel will trust my judgment. Of course, you want to get more business out of them, and they will always have more events in the future, be it parties, weddings, corporate functions, or whatever."

Often with getting gigs through an agent, the hard part is getting your foot in the door, but once you are established, you can become a reliable member of the team, much like a relief pitcher who gets sent in to get the job done, again and again. "Whether you're selling cars, tickets to a hockey game, or a band, the whole idea is to get your database to grow in both quantity and quality," Cezar says. "I wanted to have the people I worked with to trust me. You can imagine a time when four or five events later, and every time the hotel has been happy with the band that I've provided—at that point, I'm their 'go to' man."

Attitude is the key when seeing an agent. Take the time and energy to prepare your resume and come prepared. "For bands, I was always looking for professionalism. Photos, references, a resume—they were all important when meeting with an agent. Demo tapes, songs, and especially reference letters were important. If we had an event at a high-profile hotel, I would usually ask for a letter of reference if I thought it would help."

The music business is filled with artsy people who, while creatively gifted, may not have their head wrapped around the business side of things. "After I became an agent, I couldn't believe what a pain in the butt musicians were to deal with," Cezar notes. "Obviously, as a musician, I have friends in the business, but they were a real pain on some days. Most musicians out there are pretty good and reliable. But there were people out there that would drive me nuts, either by not showing up, or always being late.

"I remember once, I booked a band in Banff, Alberta, Canada, for a Friday night gig. It was for a convention. The band drove about an hour outside of Calgary. They went up in the afternoon, but the drummer was working his day job in Calgary until five o' clock that evening, and said that he would meet the band up there later. He was going to drive out to Banff in his vehicle. He ran into some car troubles and his vehicle broke down. Instead of calling anyone—me, who's the agent, anyone in the band, or the hotel in Banff where the gig was—he parked his car, walked across the highway and hitchhiked back to Calgary. He never called anyone or did anything to rectify the fact that the band in Banff now had no drummer. Fast forward a couple of hours later—the band was now up there, on stage at the hotel in Banff, without a drummer.

"The night was horrible. I could've strangled this guy. I mean, what are you thinking? Call somebody! If he would have called me, I would have got him there. Or I would have figured something out. The band could've come and got him... it was still early when he ran into car trouble. It would have been some work, but the bottom line is that the problem would have been solved. He never called anyone, or did anything."

Cezar is quick to point out that most musicians and DJs that he has worked with in the industry are respectful and courteous, but often he ran into people who were just disorganized or didn't have their life coordinated enough to be a reliable player in the industry. Note that you don't have to be a virtuoso or the world's greatest, most experienced DJ. You just have to be reliable, professional and dependable.

"There was another band that I booked regularly, and I had a lot of respect for these guys, but they were late for every gig. I mean, every single time. These guys just couldn't show up on time. Even after I had a big talk with them, it still went on. 'Guys,' I told them, 'I'm getting in trouble every Monday morning after you gig. I'm booking you guys in

Airdrie this weekend. Please don't be late."

"I was playing that same night with my own band, and I called the club in Airdrie where this other band was playing, just to make sure that they had arrived on time and were ready to go. I talked with the client; they were supposed to be playing, but they were just setting up. They were late again," Cezar notes.

"I stress that not all musicians are like that—most aren't."

DJs are, by nature, people who are interested in music and will often help create a great atmosphere at a party. However, Cezar warns that there are dangers at gigs that people in the business should be aware of. "Drugs and alcohol have been problems with musicians since before I was around, that is for sure," he says.

Make sure that you arrived prepared, with a letter of reference, photos, and a resume. If you have the attitude that you are there to work together for mutual profit, then you could be on your way to expanding your DJ business with the help of an agent.

Chapter 9:
Business & Legal Stuff

For some people, running a business is natural and relatively straightforward. Some people are great with numbers, can do their own taxes, and are not intimidated by business laws, insurance, and the general day-to-day running of an enterprise.

For others, "business" is a scary word that conjures up endless hours of doing administrative chores, shuffling paper around to make the government happy, and working really hard and hoping at the end of the day that what's left over after all of the expenses is an actual profit that can go towards bettering your life.

The good news is that if you are not naturally inclined to do some of the more "business-like" chores like taxes, that's OK. There are people out there who can help you get this stuff done. You don't need to be a Fortune 500 company in order to use an accountant, a tax preparer, or a lawyer. Let's examine some of the necessities and details of running a business.

I would like to add a short disclaimer that tax rules change and I am not a tax accountant. This advice in this book is intended as a general guideline, not as the authoritative word on business or tax law.

The Bank Account

In almost every "do-it-yourself" business book, the author always seems to say that you should get your very own bank account for your business. I disagree. The main reason for this is that the banks almost always charge you fees for business accounts. In a business account, it is not uncommon to get hit with a $10-per-month fee, plus a charge every time you make a deposit or make a withdrawal. Quite frankly, it is ridiculous for the small business owner.

These business accounts are set up with the justification that the "big corporations" eat up much of the bank's time and energy. How many checks or payments might you make in a month from your personal account? Fifteen? Twenty? Many big companies have hundreds of checks per month that are processed, plus complicated deposits are sent to the bank on a daily basis. These deposits can have numerous checks, credit card slips, or cash. Typically, big businesses do much more activity with a bank, and therefore the bank needs to charge "extra" for business accounts.

The extra charge for being a business client would be okay if you were actually a big business. But you are not (especially when you are starting out). A DJ business, even full-time, means that you might make a few deposits a week at most. If you are part-time, as many DJs are, the number is more like a couple a month.

There are many personal bank accounts set up that are no-cost, especially if you keep a minimum balance in your bank account. Some accounts, which you can find online (just google "free bank account") never charge a fee.

The important thing to remember with banking is to make sure that the customer either pays you cash or with a check that is made out to you personally (if you are not a registered company). This way, you can deposit it to the "John Smith" personal bank account instead of a high-priced "ABC DJ Company" business account.

Please note, however, that it is important to keep an accurate record of your business dealings (deposits, expenses, revenues, etc.) whether you use one bank account, two, or five. This is especially true if you are audited. Keep photocopies and records. You can never be too organized.

Registering Your Company - Municipal

You might have to register your business with the city if you are a "vendor". This means that you are selling a good or a service in the city. A business license, or a vendor's permit as it is often called, is not very expensive (usually $30-$50) and helps legitimize your business. You might get a call from a customer who saw your ad in the phone book, and if you not registered with the city or with the Better Business Bureau, you might lose that potential gig because they cannot trust that you are "legitimate".

The easiest way to check is to ask your city hall. Check out their municipal website—there is usually a "contact us" area, so just e-mail them and ask if you are not sure. Tell them that you are thinking about starting up a mobile DJ company, and ask if you need to register.

Taxes

Few things make people shudder more than taxes. However, they can be pretty straightforward and relatively easy if you *keep your receipts* and *track your revenues and expenses*. That's is the hard part—doing your taxes each spring is just a way to summarize that up for the government.

Make a spreadsheet on your computer and list the revenues from all of your gigs. It doesn't matter if people paid you cash or checks, or even work in kind, which is also known as "contra", "trade" or "barter". (An example of "work in kind" is coming up.) A good habit to get into is to be honest and list all of your revenue. It's not worth the headache to get caught cheating the government. They have much more free time and money than you or I do, so don't get in a fight with the big government agencies if you don't have to.

You might have heard people talk about "getting paid in cash" and as such they don't have to report it on their taxes. This is not true. They are cheating the tax man and could get in trouble if they are ever found out by the government. People sometimes get paid in cash because it is more difficult to track cash changing hands than a check, which is usually deposited (and recorded) by a bank.

Sample DJ Income Statement

Paper Dragon DJ Company

REVENUE

Date	Cheque	Event		Amount
July 11, 2012	25	Stampede Party	$	600.00
August 7, 2012	456	Chris Mongomeratty Wedding		550.00
September 6, 2012	34	Community Hall Speaker's Lunch		450.00
September 30, 2012	112	Hockey Team BBQ		325.00
October 31, 2012	45	Halloween Bash - Community Hall		200.00
November 10, 2012	999	Jessica Simpsonsite Wedding		600.00
		TOTAL REVENUE	**$**	**2,725.00**

Expenses

Date	Company	Expense Item		Amount
January 30, 2012	Wal-Mart	Tax Software		19.99
July 1, 2012	Mic's Mics	Microphone Stand	$	119.00
July 15, 2012	Pawn Shop	CDs - 1980s & 1990s Pop		20.00
August 1, 2012	Guitar Shop	Power Cables		82.54
August 20, 2012	Electric Store	Microphone (backup)		49.99
October 1, 2012	Fun Time News	Advertising - Local Newspaper		30.00
		TOTAL EXPENSES	**$**	**321.52**

Net Profit (Loss)			**$**	**2,403.48**

A sample Income Statement, showing revenues and expenses for the year.

Alternatively, you might wind up doing some work for "contra" or "barter". Let's say, for example, that you DJ a wedding at a golf resort for the manager's son. Instead of paying you $500 for the night, he pays you $250 and gives you 4 free rounds of golf. The golf is worth $100 per round. So, in effect, you were paid $250 cash and $400 "in kind".

You should report on your taxes $650 in income, which is the total value of the goods that you received for the services you provided. There's no difference between receiving $650 in cash, $650 in golf passes, or any combination of the two. If you don't want the golf passes, then don't accept the gig or ask for cash.

Keep your receipts. I repeat: keep your receipts. Virtually any purchase that you make in regards to your business can be deducted on your taxes. This would include the gas in your car to get to a gig, the stationary supplies that you buy (like pens, paper, business cards and paper clips), and the CDs that you purchase. You can also expense the actual computer, DJ equipment and software that you purchase (although this might be considered "capital" and would be depreciated over three years). The easiest way to handle these rules is to purchase a tax preparation CD and then you just fill in the boxes. Alternatively, you can go to a tax preparation service. Did I mention it is important to keep your receipts?

Taxes In Canada: Capital Cost Allowance

There is a term used in Canadian accounting circles called Capital Cost Allowance. It is explained by the Government of Canada at the website

www.parl.gc.ca/information/library/PRBpubs/prb0606-e.htm.

The cost of depreciable assets, such as buildings, furniture and equipment, acquired for use in business or professional activities cannot be deducted as an up-front expense when calculating net income for tax purposes. In recognition, however, of the fact that these assets wear out or become obsolete over time and are replaced, the federal government created the capital cost allowance (CCA). The CCA is a non-refundable tax deduction that reduces taxes owed by permitting the cost of business-related assets to be deducted from income over a prescribed number of years.

For example, let's pretend that in your first year of operations you were able to sell your services and bring in $15,000 in revenue.

However, you spent $3,000 on a high-end laptop computer and another $2,000 on speakers. You wouldn't just deduct the $5,000 "expenses" from your $15,000 in revenue. The reasoning behind this is that your computer and speakers will last longer than one year. This means that you spread out the expense of these items over a number of years. The length of time is determined by the government.

There are two basic terms in accounting when you purchase something—an expense is something that you use in order to run your business. Examples are gasoline, a stapler, paper, an internet connection fee—basically things that you pay for that are gone once you use them up. Usually you use them up in full in less than a year.

However, you can purchase some items that last longer than a year—much longer, in some cases. Examples of this include an automobile, a house or office, a personal computer, stereo equipment, and other equipment. These items are called "capital" as you are not merely expensing them against your revenue. You own these assets and they slowly deteriorate over time. These items are depreciated using the capital cost allowance (CCA) chart.

The government has grouped similar capital purchases into their own classes, and each of these classes has a rate in which they are depreciated over time. Computers, for example, originally fell into class 10 on the CCA schedule. This class has a 30% depreciation rate—that is, you could deduct 30% of the cost of the item against your revenue.

Recently, the government made changes for computers since they depreciate so quickly. They can now be recorded under class 45 on the CCA chart. This class has a 45% depreciation rate, which is better for the business owner because it means that they can depreciate the item quicker than before.

There is also a "half year rule" that applies to many of these CCA items. In the first year (the year of purchase), you can only deduct ½ of the value that you can in other years. So, for the first year of the computer, you could deduct 22.5% of the value, and then the next year, 45%, and then so on, until it is fully depreciated.

If all of this seems a little confusing or boring, save your receipt and go to the tax preparer at tax time and they will do the heavy lifting when it comes to this sort of thing. Usually a place like H&R Block will prepare your taxes for you for a nominal fee. However, it is always a good idea to research tax tips for your business, whether you are a consultant, freelancer, employer, or DJ. The tax preparer will only fill in the blanks on your return—they won't necessarily try to lower your taxes know every deduction that you may be eligible to make in your specific circumstance. For that, you would want to use a tax accountant, who are typically more expensive.

Keep in mind that this is just a guide; tax laws can and do change. Check Revenue Canada's website at www.cra-arc.gc.ca and make sure to read through your federal tax forms to see if there have been any changes that apply to your circumstances.

Taxes In The United States: Depreciation

The same general idea of spreading out your expenses over several years is known as depreciation in the United States. There is a great website at www.irs.gov/faqs/index.html which features frequently asked questions about U.S. taxes.

In the United States, you can claim the cost of your computer and DJ equipment is used more than 50 per cent of the time for business purposes. On your tax forms, you can use a special Code Section Election (Section 179) to expense the cost of the computer equipment all in one year (the year in which the computer is purchased and placed into service).

Generally speaking, you can claim accelerated depreciation over five tax years if the computer equipment is used more than 50% for business purposes. Keep in mind that tax laws are always changing and that this is just a guide. Check the most current IRS updates on their website (http://www.irs.gov) for specifics relating to your personal circumstances.

Registering Your Company: Trade Name

You might have heard people talk about registering their company. Should you register your company? What does that even mean? You don't need to register your company, but you might want to. Registering your company means that you pay to have the rights to a specific business name. Instead of "John Smith", someone can pay you a check made out to your company name (like "Paper Clip DJ Company") and you can cash it. Additionally, no one else can use the name "Paper Clip DJ Company", because you registered the name.

Registering your business name can be a great idea. Why not open up a restaurant and call yourself Burger King or McDonald's? Imagine all of the business you will get! You are not allowed, since those company names are already registered with the government. The companies Burger King and McDonald's already have the exclusive right to use those names. Even if your last name happens to be McDonald, you still can't use that name for your restaurant. In fact, courts might argue that you can't even use a name that is *similar* to a registered name. (I guess that MacDonald's Hamburger Restaurant is out of the question as well).

Registering your name is relatively straightforward. Check out registration search companies online or in the phone book. For a fee (about $50) the company will search their database of names in Canada or the U.S. and tell you if you can use the name. Can you imagine printing up letterhead, taking out an ad in the phone book and using business cards, only to discover that your business name "Bright Balloon DJ Services" was already registered by another person?

Even worse would be to have your company, called "Twinkle DJ" do spectacularly well for the first couple of years and then discover that someone else is using your name. You open up the newspaper one day and see an ad for "Twinkle DJ Services" but it's not your phone number or contact information! Someone else has simply stolen your business name. And since you are not registered, there's not a lot that you can do. Could you sue? If you had tons of free time and money to burn, absolutely. A little prevention at the start goes a long way to potentially avoiding headaches in some cases.

Provincial or State Tax & Goods And Services Tax

In Canada, the big question is if you should you charge GST on an event that you DJ? The answer is yes—but only if you have a GST number. You can apply for a GST number with the Government of Canada if you feel that your revenues will be over $30,000 for the year. If this is the case, then you must put your GST number on the invoices that you provide, and you must keep track of it and remit it to the government (usually quarterly). You also get to claim GST on any expenses that you incur where you pay GST. If you buy a CD for ten dollars, for example, and you actually pay $10.50, then you would get to claim back 50 cents on your GST return. You wind up paying the net of what you remit (on earnings) and claim (on expenses).

For most part-timers, it's not worth the time and trouble to collect GST on your goods and services, especially if you are not earning more than $30,000 a year on your business income. However, if you start getting close to this amount, apply for a number—if you earn $30,001, you need to remit GST on the *whole amount* earned for the year.

In the United States and Canada, the rule on sales tax is simple - you should charge it and remit it. Of course, each state and province is different, so check your state or provincial government's website to make sure that you have met the requirements. It really isn't difficult; you just fill out a form and keep track of your sales. Charge the client the percentage of sales tax that is applicable to your state or province. (If you are not sure what the percentage is, look it up online, or simply go to the mall and purchase something—it will be on the receipt.)

How Much Do You Charge?

How much money can you make as a DJ? This is the burning question that new DJs have when they start out. After buying a computer, DJ equipment and a thousand songs, you have laid out some serious money. How long before you can recoup it and make a profit?

It totally depends on the services that you are providing, the market that you are in, and the demand for your services. High-end DJs who offer full wedding services (like acting as emcee and basically "running the show" for the entire evening) can charge well over $1,000 a night for their services. Some DJ companies also offer video services in addition to their musical services, which means that while the party is grooving, the camera is rolling. In addition to a great night of music and an emcee, your client gets a wedding memento as well—a videotape or DVD of them and their friends dancing up a storm, cutting the cake, and even making speeches—all the special moments that will be captured by you.

Other DJ companies provide the bare bones. They show up with a couple of speakers, some songs, and a microphone, and they spin tunes and do it very well. But that's all they do. In these instances, you can charge $200 a night and up. Although this may sound a less glamorous, the chances of you getting paying clients (especially at the start) increases dramatically with a "basic service" package. There are many people who want to have a DJ but cannot afford a luxurious high-end package. One is not better than the other; they are just simply different types of clients.

For Christmas and New Year's Eve, the law of supply and demand kicks in and you can charge more for these high-demand nights. Weekends (Friday and Saturday nights) should be more expensive than other nights of the week. Many part-time DJs do not even offer services during the week, because they are working their day jobs.

The easiest way to see what others charge for their services is to go online and check out some DJ companies. See if they post their prices. If they don't, phone them up and ask them how much they charge. Don't tell them that you are starting up your own DJ company; rather, tell them that you are pricing out a wedding reception, stag party, community hall event, or office party and want to see what they offer and how much they charge (only pick one event when you are phoning or else you are going to sound like a lazy researcher and may not get any answers). Once you have that information from a few DJ companies, charge a little bit less than they do when you are starting out. If you charge a little less and offer a little more, you are stacking the odds in your favor of becoming very successful.

Refundable Deposit

You are going to run into a super high-maintenance customer, or some event in your life will transpire that will cause you or the client to cancel an event. That's just the way life works. You might suffer a death in the family, or an illness, or some other important event that means that you will not be able to DJ an event.

If you can't get a replacement, then explain to the customer that you are sorry and refund their money. Of course, it goes without saying that you should do everything in your power to DJ the event if you are physically able to do it. After all, a few scorched gigs here and there has a way of breeding a bad reputation, and that's something that you don't need in the business world.

When the customer fills out and signs the contract, they should include a deposit, like $100 or so. If the customer cancels the event, you keep the money. They are paying you money to hold that date in your calendar. Like most DJs, especially when starting out, you will only have one set of speakers, one computer, and one person DJing—you. If people can cancel anytime, and without penalty, then you are doing a lot of work and getting little reward.

If, however, something really important comes up and you need to cancel, refund the customer's money promptly and apologize. Be honest about why you are unable to commit to the dance or party and hopefully they will understand. You might even want to have a replacement (a different DJ business) that you can recommend as a second choice for the customer.

Insurance

The only thing worse than someone spilling a rum & Coke on your $2,000 laptop is not having any insurance to cover it. You probably already deal with an insurance company now, if you own your own home, rent, or operate a motor vehicle. If that is the case, just give them a call and explain that you have a few thousand dollars of DJ equipment and that you are thinking about getting some insurance. There are a few different types of insurance, and the major ones are listed below.

Business Interruption: If you have a disaster and cannot operate your business, this insurance pays you for salaries, taxes, rents, and net profits that would have been earned during the period in question.

Liability: This type of insurance covers injuries that you may cause to a third party, such as a person on the dance floor. If someone sues you for damages, this insurance would cover the cost of the lawsuit. A general liability policy will cover you against most accidents that may occur while doing a gig.

Crime / Theft: This is the obvious one. If someone steals your equipment, you are covered by the insurance policy. Make sure to save your receipts from your purchases and even take photographs of your expensive equipment.

Insurance can be very detailed and can involve a lot of time and energy. Do your homework and get a basic liability policy that protects you from a lawsuit. Also get a theft policy so that if someone rips off your equipment, it's not the end of your business. These two are the critical types of insurance for peace of mind. Shop around and see who offers what rates. Insurance can be very personal, so match up your needs with the prices that are offered.

Getting Paid

Is it rude to ask for money up front? What happens if you DJ all night and then, when it is time to ask for the money, the bride and groom's parents have left the reception hall? These questions were forefront in my mind when I DJ'd my first few gigs.

I always made sure to get a $100 deposit. This way, even in the absolute worst circumstances, I at least had $100 in my pocket before the event even began. You might run into some bar owners who are rather shady, but for the most part, the corporate clients, like those who are having Christmas parties, weddings and community hall parties, are happy and able to pay you.

That having been said, however, make sure that you get paid before the wee hours of the morning. Chances are good that most people at weddings are drinking, and there is loud music, strobe lights, and lots of people around. That is not the best time to ask for payment.

Bring the contract with you. Keep it in your back pocket. Sometimes the client will forget how much they owe. Did you say $250 or $350? Remember, they are paying caterers and other event staff as well as you, so don't be surprised if it completely slips their mind. I always take it as a compliment when the client forgets to pay me—it means that I was doing such a great job that he or she wasn't even thinking about me!

I usually make a point to ask for the money about halfway through the event. This way, if they are not happy with a certain part of the event, you will find out about it before the end of the night and have a chance to fix the problems. If you don't discover that the client is unhappy until the end of the evening when you are packing up your gear and the guests are making their way to the door, then there is nothing you can do to remedy the situation. Finding out about bad sound or song selections with a few hours left in the evening will usually help you fix the problem and create another happy client.

Employees

At the start, you will probably want to DJ all of the gigs yourself. After all, you got into this business to mix songs, party and make some money. There might come a time, however, when your business has grown to the point where you are turning down gigs. This usually happens at the Christmas season (November and December) and it can be frustrating because you won't have any action for the whole week, and then you will have two clients both willing to pay you for a Saturday night party.

If this happens, you can do one of two things: don't sweat it and turn down the gig, or hire a subcontractor and have your business perform both gigs. Subcontractors are independent business people just like you. However, they will be working for you for this one gig only, and then they will no longer be performing services for you (until the next gig, of course).

This is different than an employee. An employee enters into a relationship with their employer (you) and you have to pay them, even if there is no business. You also have much more responsibility as an employer, such as withholding taxes and payroll taxes. Avoid all of those hassles and just hire someone as a subcontractor for one night's work!

You might be surprised at how easy it is to hire a subcontractor. Do you have any friends who would be interested in DJing? You probably have some buddies who are interested in making some good money for a few hours work, and if you buy a second set of equipment, then you not only have a quality backup set of gear but are also ready to take on two gigs.

Let's use the following example of how subcontracting works. If a client phones and wants you to work a Saturday night corporate gig, and you accept and have agreed to a $400 payday, then you are all set. But wait! The phone rings only minutes later and another group wants to hire you for the same Saturday night! They are also willing to pay you $400. Now you are sweating. Why couldn't their gig be the following Saturday? But it's not. You now have two gigs on the same night. You place a quick call to your friend and offer him the Saturday night gig. He agrees readily, since he is using your equipment and will make a cool $250 for a few hours work.

That means that you will make $400 from your client on Saturday night, plus your friend will also get paid $400. But he'll hand over $150 at the end of the night to you, since you are the owner of the business, it's all your gear, and your friend did no advertising, research or marketing. He just showed up and made $250. It's a great deal for him and a great deal for you.

Chapter 10:
Marketing & Advertising

Some people might think that every business starts with advertising or marketing. Why do all this work if you can't find any customers?

It's true that the most important part of any business isn't the hardware or software, or even the employees or hard work. The most important part of any successful business is the sale. You can also substitute the word "customer" or "client" in there instead, but make no mistake: the most important part of the business is the actual sale that brings in money to the business. Without it, everything else is just hard work and effort without any reward. A business without sales is just a hobby.

I mention this because it is important that when your business becomes hours and hours of research, recording and remixing songs, playing and replaying mp3 files, scanning the bargain bins at the music stores for the latest CDs, talking with other DJs and spending your hard-earned money on DJ equipment, microphone stands and advertising, you need to sometimes remind yourself that it's all with one goal in mind: bring in the money.

It's very important as well to enjoy your job or your business and to feel fulfilled in life. However, we are not talking about a hobby or a pastime. If you want your DJ business to be successful, you need customers, clients, sales and money. Cash is king.

Phases Of Business - Marketing vs. Advertising

Like many successful businesses in the world, there are three different phases that you will hopefully go through. The first is the setup phase, when you are basically setting up shop and waiting for the phone to ring. Your energy is high and your client list is small. Once you get some regular, successful gigs under your belt, and your business is firmly established, you will hopefully really enjoy the work and want to grow it. This means getting a referral list that is ever-growing, slowly increasing your fees as your experience increases and your ability to handle different types of events grow. The third stage arrives when you have so much business that you are actually turning down gigs. This means either that you have achieved your goals and you can take a sip of champagne in-between the chaos of a constantly ringing phone, or it means that you might want to think about expanding your business and hiring subcontractors.

Remember to dream big but start small. You are building a business and that means that you want to draw on a solid foundation. You need to have the skills in place to successfully expand.

The main reason for describing the three phases of businesses is that the type of advertising that you do depends on two things: the size of your business and the goal of the advertising.

The very first step when setting out an advertising strategy is marketing. Marketing is the research that goes on before the advertising. Marketing is the process of determining who the customer is and what their needs are.

Not all customers are the same. As you've seen throughout this book, there are many different types of gigs and events. Which types do you think you can handle the best and why? Are there certain types of events that you will enjoy doing more than others? These factors should play a role in determining how best to serve your customers.

Remember that you have a choice on whether to offer "low-end" services, which is essentially a bare-bones DJ service at a very low price, and the "high-end" service, which will cost the client much more but will include many additional features, such as lights, emcee services, and more powerful speakers. You can also tackle all of these segments by offering up different packages for different types of events. Clients can pick from a menu, just like when they order a pizza and select their favorite toppings.

It might be great that you want to be a "high-end" provider or a "low-end" provider, but the other part of the marketing research is determining whether your services would be in demand. Take a look in the phone book. Are there a ton of different DJ services? Are there any? Are they mostly high-end or low-end? What services do they offer? If you go to a Christmas party or a wedding, check out the DJ booth. Are they blowing you away with all the terrific services that they provide? Or is it a bare-bones approach by the guy who looks bored and unmotivated?

There are four areas to research when creating a marketing plan. The first two are internal and the last two are external. *Internal* means that the research pertains to your business. *External* means that the research pertains to the environment outside your business. You have the power to control the internal items, but the external ones often fall outside your realm of influence.

The two internal factors in a marketing plan are your strengths and your weaknesses. What do you enjoy doing? Are you good at it? For example, you might have vast and extensive knowledge of the music on all of your CDs. But can you emcee a wedding? Maybe you are technically proficient at the actual beat mixing and remixing of songs, but you are horribly shy. Size up your strengths and your weaknesses. It would help to physically write them down.

The two external factors are threats and opportunities. These are the situations and realities that fall outside of your business. Examples of opportunities are areas of DJ entertaining that perhaps are not being serviced. Maybe there is a shortage of DJs in the area. Or perhaps there are five high-priced DJs and no reliable low-priced ones. The threats are the areas of the industry that can negatively affect your business. Perhaps there are many competitors or your town has very seasonal gigs. Are there ways that you can branch out your business, based on your strengths?

If you can minimize the external threats and maximize your external opportunities by using your strengths, while at the same time work towards minimizing or eliminating your weaknesses, then you are heads and shoulders above your competition and should be stacking the odds in your favor to succeed.

What does any of this have to do with advertising? The short answer is that advertising is more than just shouting to the world "I'm here". Successful advertising will make the customer want to purchase your services and feel great about doing it. Marketing is the process of finding the questions that consumer ask ("Where is a reasonable priced DJ?" or "Does anyone DJ graduation ceremonies?"). Advertising is the process of answering those questions.

For start-up businesses and small businesses, you probably won't be doing much in the way of big advertising. Remember, advertising can be very expensive. What follows is a breakdown of different types of advertising. There is no right way to advertise. However, you want to make sure that your advertising dollars are an investment rather than a cost. For example, if you spend $500 on a huge billboard in your city and it creates zero sales, that is not an effective use of your money. However, if you spend $500 on a huge billboard and get five $250 gigs out of it, that could be seen as a good return on your $500 investment. Ever wonder why some customer questionnaires ask "how did you hear about us"? They track the use of their advertising and monitor how effective their ad campaigns are. Whether you are a multi-million-dollar corporation or a one-man operation working out of your basement, advertising goals are the same: to get sales.

Let's start with the smallest start-up business scenario and see if there are some low-cost ways to get your name out in to the public eye.

Advertising For Small Businesses

For small businesses, or any business for that matter, you want to have the most effective and efficient marketing plans. *Effective* advertising is the basically a measure of the result. If your goal is to advertise and increase your sales by $2,000 over the holiday season, and you actually get $500 total, then your campaign was not very effective. If, on the other hand, you get $4,000 business out of your specific advertising, then you would conclude that the advertising campaign was effective.

Effective advertising is directly related to your goals. Make sure that you have some goals! In most cases, you will want to track your spending on advertising and see if it generates more business than it costs to produce. This leads us to the next marketing term: efficiency.

What is an efficient marketing campaign? *Efficiency* is the measure of the output compared to the input. For example, imagine a runner and a cyclist moving along a long, flat, steady highway. If the runner spends 1,000 calories running, and the guy on the bicycle spends 1,000 calories on the bike, who is going to go further?

Naturally, the cyclist is going to travel more distance while using the same energy. Besides, when he's done spending his energy, he could probably coast for quite a while without spending any energy! This makes sense, since the cyclist has a mechanical advantage over the runner. The idea is similar in the world of advertising.

If the cyclist travels 5,000 yards while spending 1,000 calories, then his efficiency rating would be 5. (5,000 divided by 1,000). If the runner can get 2,000 yards done while spending the same amount of energy, then his efficiency rating would be 2 (2,000 divided by 1,000). The cyclist was two and a half times more efficient—that is, the cyclist covered more ground using the same energy.

How does this affect the DJ? The best way (translation: the way with the lowest cost) to get your name out there is to use low-cost or no-cost advertising at the start. Then, as your business grows, consider using more expensive advertising, tracking how much business it is able to generate.

The best advertising is word-of-mouth advertising. The best way to increase your word-of-mouth advertising is to do a great job when you DJ. Make sure to leave DJ business cards on the tables at the wedding and/or at the bar. For weddings, have a little baggie of candies sitting on the table with a business card attached. This ensures that a least some people notice the card! Hopefully, if you are doing a great job, people will take the DJ card from one of the tables. Sometimes people will come up to the DJ and ask them for a business card. Have them on the corner of the table for easy access. Make it easy for potential clients to remember who you are and how to get in touch with you.

A website is another great way to increase awareness. Spend the $10 a month to get a "real" website, not a freebie one with a ton of advertising. If you get a website domain through Yahoo! or some other major search engine or website provider, they will make sure that your services are listed in their search engine. If someone types in "Etobicoke DJ" or wherever you live, your DJ page will be near the top of the list.

One more note about business cards—always carry them around with you and always give them out whenever you can. Business cards are really inexpensive and it has all of your contact info on there. You can buy thousands of business cards for $20 or $30. Make sure that they don't just sit on a shelf somewhere—get them in the hands of potential customers. This includes the manager of the hotel or ballroom where you just worked. Give them out to the manager and they might give you a call when they are in a bind (for example, their regular DJ didn't show up for a gig) or even if a client sees the hotel and wants to hire a DJ.

Here are some various brainstorming ideas that won't cost much money. Of course, there are endless possibilities, so pick what you like and give some a try. You don't have to do any of these—you may have more gigs can you can handle just from word of mouth! Remember, if you do try any of these (or other) marketing ideas, make sure to monitor your results and see which ones worked for you.

- Sponsor a youth sports team in your community.
- Rent your sound system to fashion shows, malls, stores, etc.

- Paint your company logo and advertisement on the side of your van or truck. Also, put magnetic signs on the sides of all of your mobile entertainer's vehicles.

- Print T-shirts with your company logo and website.

- Send a direct mail flyer or fax to local businesses for their company holiday party.

- Place ads on the church bulletin boards around your community. Bar and Bat mitzvahs, church BBQs and community parties are great ways to meet and greet members of the community.

- Offer to work a charity event as a volunteer. You get free advertising and experience and it goes to a good cause.

- Send press releases to newspapers and trade publications.

- Give catering halls stickers or fridge magnets with your company name, website and phone number.

- Offer a commission to catering halls that recommend you. Provide them with cards and brochures.

- Perform at bridal shows, conventions, trade shows and exhibitions.

- Place your cards and flyers on bulletin boards. (colleges, the grocery store, Laundromats, the library, bowling alleys, etc.)

- Sign up on social networking sites like Facebook and Twitter. Keep your site active with updates and information.

- Start a blog and keep it fun, informative and up to date.

Advertising For Medium Businesses

Hopefully you have been using the "small business" advertising techniques and some of them have paid off. As the gigs increase in both frequency and pay checks, the big question is going to be "how to I take it to the next level?"

This is the most tricky part of the business phase, because you are going to be making money and getting the green eyes. You will want more! However, some advertising out there is really expensive and you have to make sure that any money you spend is going to work for you.

Usually the next step involves putting an advertisement in the phone book (if it still exists in your area). You will want to first call the phone company and purchase a separate line just for your DJ business. If you don't and you wind up using your home phone number as the listed DJ number, then what happens if a potential client phones your number because they got it out of the phone book? They will either get "hello", which is completely unprofessional, or they will get your answering machine, which will sound like someone's personal answering machine ("Hi, you've reached Steve and I'm not able to come to the phone right now,") because that is what it is. Alternatively, you don't want to have "ABC DJ Company" on your personal answering machine, because anyone leaving you a personal voice message might get confused. The simple solution is to buy a separate phone line, get a separate phone and answering machine, and put them in your home office.

For many DJs, this will be enough. The $200 per year of a dedicated phone line and answering machine will probably result in some increased business, because your phone line may get an automatic placement in the phone book. Just make sure that you are listed under "DJ" or "disc jockey" and you are all set.

Inquire about all the different types of advertising that you can do in the phone book. For example, you might be able to have your business line listed without an ad, but with your website right next to the number. This will probably be much less expensive than if you buy a ¼ page ad, which can run into hundreds if not thousands of dollars.

It's important when buying advertising vehicles that people have a way to get in contact with you. This means putting your easy-to-remember phone number or website on coffee mugs, T-shirts, fridge magnets and stickers.

At the actual gig, make sure to have a small and classy sign visible to guests. It only needs to be about 2-feet high by 3-feet wide and have "tonight's entertainment brought to you by The Rusty Cage DJ Company" (or whatever you are calling yourself). This is a one-time cost since you can use the sign over and over again. Get it professionally printed. It will be worth the cost. The sign should be unobtrusive so that wedding guests and clients will hardly notice it if they are not looking for it, but anyone who is wondering who the DJ is will be able to figure it out quickly.

Another great idea for advertising your business is a car magnet. You can get them to fit the sides of your car or truck (usually on the doors). When you get your automobile washed, you can just take them off and reapply them later. These are low-cost ways of advertising, as you will be driving around the city anyway to buy groceries and get your daily chores done—why not let people know about your DJ services too!

There might be a small, independent radio station in your city or town that is looking for volunteers. If so, it could be an excellent way to promote your skills as a DJ. Working at the radio station for even a couple of hours per month means that you can add that skill and experience to your resume or your website, and clients will see that you are a "real DJ". You might even become a local celebrity and that will almost automatically command a higher price for gigs. You may be able to mention your DJ services while you are working on the radio. You never know where that next client is going to come from.

Advertising For Big Businesses

How do you know when you are a "big business"? There is not really set answer for this, but generally speaking, you are "big" or "established" when you are no longer in the startup mode, you have a steady stream of customers, and you are actually turning down gigs because the demand is so high.

If you are turning down paying gigs, why on earth would you advertise? That is a great question, and many DJ companies don't advertise. For example, can you name the three biggest DJ companies in your city? Probably not, and I can guarantee that the average person looking for a DJ company for a wedding is not going to have heard of any of the companies, ever, unless they are offshoots of existing music stores, television stations or local radio stations.

Advertising at this stage is only necessary if you are interested in pursuing higher-end clients who want to purchase more than the bare-bones DJ services. For example, you might want to partner up with an emcee, a rock band, or a party planning company and co-promote your services. Or you may have expanded the services that you offer to include these and you want to make people aware. Either way, you would want to update or expand your website in this case, and you might also want to look at higher-end brochures or phone book advertising.

Usually at this point, you have a decision to make: do you continue to expand your services, add on employees and increase your advertising? Or do you continue to work full-time at DJing, turning down occasional gigs? It is a tough call, and only you can make that decision. There's an old saying that no one ever goes broke by selling out of an item. In other words, if you are running at full capacity and cannot handle any more business, then you might be happy with that and will enjoy the fruits of your labor. For others, they want to be the boss and have a small army of DJs working gigs all over the city. There is no right answer, but the important thing to remember is that every time you spend money on equipment, staff, advertising or supplies, ask yourself "how will this expense result in sales? How will it increase my profit? How will this investment pay me back?"

The Club DJ

Advertising for the club DJ is a completely different ballgame in some areas, but very similar in others. Again, it's all about making the sale or getting the gig. For the club DJ, you are actually advertising yourself, rather than your services. It is similar to a rock band or a singer. The club will want to hire you in the hopes that paying customers will walk in the club to see you perform.

Your advertising should be based more toward club owners and managers rather than the average consumer walking the streets. Once you have a paying gig, however, consider putting up posters and flyers advertising the event. You want to be able to march up to the owner after the event and have him know that it was because of your talent and promotions that the house was packed!

As your business grows, you will want to actively promote your name. If you get to the point that you are in high demand, start increasing your fees. This could be the most difficult of the whole process, because some bar owners and nightclub managers are notoriously cheap and might turn down your offer. If that is the case, make sure to walk away. You must stand your ground. It's a tough call because on the one hand, you want to work and earn money, but on the other hand, if you are becoming more popular and more in demand, you must follow the money trail and that ultimately leads to higher fees. You will only get paid what you ask for—never more.

One way to avoid pricing yourself out of a job is competing offers. If you have a gig at the local nightclub for the next four weekends, honor your contract, but increase your fee slightly and shop around to other bars and clubs. After your gig, you might find that your next one is for five weekends at a higher rate. Then go back to the first nightclub in a couple of months and if they offer you the same original contract, you can show him that you are commanding a higher rate at a competing bar. That might get them to play ball.

For really popular DJs, the money can be amazing. There are DJs who command thousands of dollars for a few hours' work on the weekend. Make sure to build your brand slowly, be really good at what you do, and aim high.

Conclusion:
Get Going!

What you have just read are ten crucial steps to go from a dream into a reality. Of course, reading a book is just part of the research that you will do, and research is just the start of your journey in the business world. Or, alternatively, you already have a DJ business and you are looking for ways to increase sales, get more fulfillment out of the business and expand. Either way, I hope that you have found the steps listed here helpful, educational and sound.

The average nine-to-fiver will never get rich, and they will never do what they want to do in life. If you look at all of the super-rich people in today's society—people like Bill Gates, Warren Buffet and local businessmen, it is obvious that the road to becoming a millionaire means investing wisely, having a really strong work ethic and working for yourself.

No one can promise you riches, but being a DJ will give you the potential to make some good money. The beauty of working for yourself is that you not only get to keep all the money you earn, but you have literally an unlimited potential for profit, growth and success.

So what is holding you back? There's an old joke that university graduates work really hard for a manager who barely finished high school. The manager works hard for the owner. And the owner is the guy who dropped out of high school and started up his own business.

This is not always true—not by a long shot. However, it does illustrate that sometimes in life it is more important to take a risk and actually do it than to sit around and wonder about it. You will never be able to fully research anything completely—ultimately you need to get out there and do it.

What's the best way to get started in the DJ business? The safest way would be to start out on a part-time basis. Keep your day job. Your regular job provides a steady source of income and some stability in your life. If you are working a job on the weekends, try to get a job that you can go to during the week. This will free up your Friday nights and weekends, when 95% of the DJ gigs occurs.

Maybe you are scared about making mistakes. I know I was. When I was starting out, I was so nervous before my first few DJ gigs that I couldn't sleep the night before the event. I remember one barbeque that I DJ'd and the event planner graciously offered up a huge steak and potato dinner, complete with vegetables, drinks, and desert. I reluctantly picked at my steak and sipped my water—I was way too nervous to eat.

So what if you make a few mistakes? The important thing is that you learn from them. I definitely made mistakes along the way, and that is why I wrote this book. I wanted to illustrate that these mistakes are normal and hopefully you won't repeat them. However, I guarantee that you DJ, you will make some other mistakes at some point. It's just not that big of a deal, as long as you go into it with an excited and professional attitude. Remember, you are also going to do some exciting and cool things as a DJ that will make hundreds of people have a fantastic evening!

I've illustrated some key points below that you can use as a road map to becoming a successful DJ:

- Go see a wedding, party or event from the eyes of a DJ. Sit near the music and pay attention to what the DJ is playing and why. Take notes if you feel that will help.

- Look online for some free DJ software. Download it and learn how to use it. Have some fun with it!

- Go to three different music stores and price out a basic set of speakers and a mixer. Take your laptop computer with you and plug it in. For a thousand-dollar (or more) sale, don't be afraid to test drive the equipment.

- Get business cards printed up—and actually hand them out.

- If you are having trouble getting gigs, ask around and offer to DJ an event for free. It could be a community event, a friend's party, the company Christmas party, or any event where music is played. It's very hard for a client to get angry if you are providing services for no money. Get a reference letter if they are happy with your work.

- Spend a weekend looking at DJ websites. Make notes of what services they offer, and what services you would like to provide.

- Phone or email DJ businesses to find out prices (if they are not listed on their website). Ask them what they charge and what that includes. If they ask who you are, just say that you are thinking about having a wedding or hosting a party.

- Make sure to tell your friends and family that you are a DJ. People are always getting married or having parties, reunions, etc.

- If you can afford it, put an ad online (it used to be the phone book, but now there are online directories) or get a dedicated phone number for your DJ business and have it listed.

- Print up some flyers and send them to community halls, wedding planners, churches, businesses, community associations, and whoever else you think would host a party.

Your business will probably grow by repeat business, word of mouth and advertising. You will find that it is much easier to get repeat business from some clients, as some committees and hosts don't really want to spend hours researching DJs. Once you have proven to them that you are professional and reliable, they will probably book you for each annual gig (like a yearly community party, a Christmas party, or some similar event).

Word-of-mouth advertising is great, primarily because it is free. Once word is out that you are professional and good at what you do, the phone will start ringing and the e-mails will start arriving. Make sure to have plenty of business cards with you and hand them out whenever you get a chance.

Advertising can be really, really expensive. Some businesses, such as Costco, have achieved major sales over the years with virtually no advertising. You can do that as well. Keep your advertising costs low. Think about who is going to need your services. You are not going to attract an "impulse" buyer, so don't bother with visual advertising like signs, billboards, bus benches, and the like. Create a website and make sure it is easy to navigate. People who are looking for a DJ in Toronto will Google "DJ Toronto". Make sure you are available to your web customers—if someone e-mails you and inquires about your services, respond quickly and be helpful. They will also look up "Disc Jockey" in the phone book. Have your number listed and that alone will result in inquiries and eventually sales. Generally speaking, the most important thing to remember is that every dollar you spend in advertising could be money in your pocket. So spend it wisely. Don't bother advertising to regions that you can't actually service. For example, don't even bother looking at advertising in a provincial or national newspaper or magazine. What's the point? A business in New York or Vancouver cannot perform DJ services in each other's vicinity, so don't bother spending that kind of money. Start with the basics (like business cards, flyers or letters to prospective businesses and event halls, and a listed phone number under "DJ Services").

Many coaches and corporate speakers are paid big money to motivate their athletes, employees or team members. If you are working for yourself, the only person who will truly motivate you is you. The first step is to visualize what success means for you personally. Do you want to have a huge DJ empire? Or would you be happy with lots of free time and only working three days a week? Do you picture your business with an assistant, some DJ employees, and you sitting in the big chair, securing paying gigs? Do you want an office? Or will you be working out of your house?

There are no right or wrong answers. The old saying that "time is money" is really true. Some people would love a huge business and working their passion 60 or 70 hours a week. They can imagine themselves retiring as a millionaire at forty-five or fifty years of age and going to the beach or the golf course. Other entrepreneurs would rather work part-time, and earn some good money doing it. Their goals involve doing other things with their lives, and they don't necessary want to work many hours in the week. Many people are a combination of the two—after all, I think every person would like more money and more free time!

Once you have your "big picture" dream, break it out into a plan. How are you going to get from where you are right now to where you want to be? The most important part of the whole process is the actual sale, or gig. Without that, you are just running around for free. Most DJs at the start will take any gig, and especially any paying gig. It not only gets you a contact and experience, but also some money.

Motivation is key, especially at the start. The world is full of people who never abandon the safety of their routine to try something new. Again, this is not necessarily a bad thing for everyone. Not every person is cut out to be a business owner. Your work as an entrepreneur may not pay dividends right at the start. If you take a full-time job, for example, and you work 40 hours in a week, you will most certainly get paid for 40 hours' worth of work. But as a business owner, you may work 60 hours a week for the first three months and not see any return at all. You can't force people to pick up the phone or send you an e-mail. However, there is a flip side, and that is that if your business becomes successful, you could be generating income without having to work at all.

Imagine, for example, if you had a DJ business with three mobile DJs who worked corporate events, and two club DJs. A client phones you, and they want a DJ to work a trade show on the outskirts of town and are willing to pay your company $500 a night for three nights. You accept, talk to one of your DJ employees (or sub-contractors) and he agrees to take the gig. "You can count on me boss," he says, and the show is a big hit. The check arrives for $1,500, and your business takes $500 and you pay the DJ $1,000 for three nights' work.

Let's recap: you just answered the phone, talked to one person, and then banked $500. Sound too easy? It happens. It happens all the time. Remember, growing a business is like building a garden. You work really hard at the beginning cultivating the garden, and then when the fruit blossoms, you can enjoy it. Don't ever stop trying to grow and nourish your garden!

Keep your eye on the prize: money. You are starting up a business and want to make sales, earn revenue, and ultimately make a profit. Whether it is making enough money to someday quit your day job and do this full time, or it is part-time fun on the weekend a few times a year, the successful businesses are the ones that close sales and perform actual paying gigs. Holding meetings, dressing up in a fancy suit, and spending countless hours cataloguing your songs are all "playing businessman". Don't play it. Be it. That means putting money in the bank.

Make sure to surround yourself with successful and positive people. You don't need to listen to nay-Sayers and doubters. Be open to criticism and advice, but don't be open to negative people who want to see you fail.

Start small and dream big. Those are the two most important ideals to create your own successful DJ business. Good luck!

Appendix 1:
Case Study – 20/20

Dan Cezar has been in music business for almost 40 years. As the bass player for the band 20/20, he has played all sorts of venues, from tiny weddings in community halls to huge outdoor tailgate parties for the Calgary Flames during their 2003 / 2004 NHL Stanley Cup run.

Cezar also looked after the business side of things with the band. He was responsible for booking the majority of the events that 20/20 performed, as well as securing payment from clients and writing thank-you notes. Once a week the band met at his south Calgary home, where they worked on learning new songs, perfecting older ones, trying out new arrangements, discussing upcoming events, and generally handling the day-to-day activities of being in a working band.

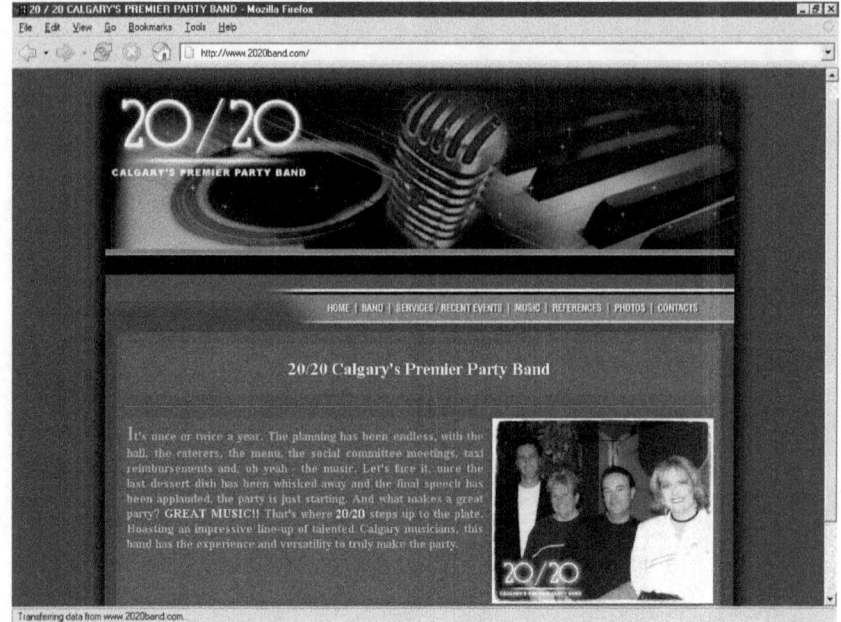

*20 / 20 was a Calgary-based band that performed all across Canada.
Here is their website's homepage from their touring days.*

"Having a website really helped our band," notes Cezar. "I
remember hearing about a gentleman from Chicago. He typed in
'Calgary Party Band' online and found our website. He was looking for
a band who played in the same city where his daughter lived. So he liked
what he saw and gave me a call. He wanted to know if we were
available to play a wedding. He wanted to hear what we sounded like. I
told him that we had demo songs on our website. He could listen to the
band right online. We were available on the date that we was looking
for, and the next thing you know we were booked for a wedding."

Cezar notes that for a DJ or a band looking to promote themselves, a
website really speeds up the process—you can see what the band looks
like, sounds like, and even peruse recent gigs and reference letters. "For
a potential customer in another city or country to be able to get all that

information and book the band within an hour—that is truly something special. I faxed over a contract, and he signed it and faxed it right back. Done deal."

Their website, originally found online at www.2020band.com, was quite extensive. It featured band photos, a short biography on each member of the band, song clips, and a menu of songs that the band knew and could play.

"One thing I stressed with my band members was that we were there to do what the client wanted, not necessarily what we wanted," Cezar notes. He has learned over 100 songs throughout his long music career and remembers that many of the tunes that the band played were not his personal favorites.

"I've worked with many DJs in the past, as many events call for both the band and a DJ. I've seen many DJs walk in and figure that they are going to play what they want, not what the client would like to hear. It doesn't quite work that way. There's going to be music in there that you are not thrilled about playing. The bottom line, however, is that if the music works, and the client is happy, and the dance floor is filled, then you should be happy as well."

For DJs, Cezar suggests that reference letters are key. "I would think that a DJ should have reference letters from all high-profile clients. They should have a couple of wedding party references, a couple of corporate references, and a couple of other references, like sporting events or community hall parties. For any high-profile event, try to get a reference letter."

Cezar has been both a bass player in a band and also a music agent, booking events for other bands and DJs when his own band was already booked for the night in question. "I've found that most agents are open to meeting with DJs and bands, provided that you are prepared and professional," he notes. "Most agents are very busy people, so the meeting will not be very long. But I think it is reasonable to meet with an agent for five or ten minutes, introduce yourself, and drop off a package that includes your credentials, what services you provide, your price list, and reference letters. If you are serious about it, be persistent. Call back. There are plenty of agents out there, so if you run into one or two that are not very friendly, then move on and find one that you can get excited about working with."

The Calgary Exhibition & Stampede is one of the biggest events in all of western Canada—thousands of people visit the Stampede grounds each day during its run and people all across North America tune in to watch the world-class rodeo on television. 20/20 has enjoyed a recurring Stampede corporate event that has lasted now over twenty years. Although 20/20 does not actively tour anymore, they still play the Calgary Stampede. "It was first booked through an agent back in the 1980s," Cezar notes. "The Stampede picked this agent and asked him to provide a band for the caravan gig, and he called us." The Calgary Exhibition & Stampede, through the caravan, generates a community-minded, family-oriented presence throughout Calgary. The caravan travels to large malls in Calgary during the Stampede and offers family-oriented entertainment to shoppers.

"The caravan is like a mini-Stampede," notes Cezar. "We go to all the big malls in Calgary, and it lasts all ten days during the Stampede. It usually runs from nine until eleven in the morning. It's a great way for the Stampede to show their goodwill to the community. With the help of about 120 volunteers, they set up a huge Stampede breakfast. We come out, play about three or four songs, and then they have other entertainment for people, such as Native Indian dancers, mini-dog shows, and other family entertainment."

Cezar notes that the Caravan event, like many of the corporate gigs, involve playing to families and passersby, as well as waiting around. "We always have to be ready, because once the other entertainment is over, we would go back on and play another mini-set," explains Cezar. "We can't really leave the stage and go wander around, since we only have about sixty seconds to get playing once the people are done giving their speech, or dancing, or whatever the show is before we come on. The show really caters to families and kids. There are mascots and rodeo clowns out there mingling in the crowd, and there are lots of activities for the little guys."

Corporate gigs are very safe and controlled, and they can be very lucrative, notes Cezar, who has not only worked the Calgary Exhibition & Stampede, but has also worked functions in conjunction with the Canadian Football League's Grey Cup and the National Hockey League's Calgary Flames. "I personally like corporate gigs a lot more than playing in bars," notes Cezar, "although everyone will have their own personal preference."

Cezar is quick to point out the benefits of working corporate events—usually the clients are nice and they always pay their bill. That doesn't always happen in bars. "I worked over ten years in the bar scene—I've found that lots of bars can be shady. It can be smoky (although that is now changing), sometimes it is not as safe, the money is much less lucrative than a typical corporate event, and the pressure is on. If it's a Friday night, and you are in the bar playing, and the people aren't coming in—you might take heat over that. Is it your responsibility to bring people into the bar? The owner might think it is."

Corporate events can feature a very different clientele. "You are catering to a very specific client at corporate events and usually play toned-down, very safe music. In a bar, you can play some of your own songs, or jazz it up, or do whatever you like on some nights. Playing a corporate event usually means playing very popular cover tunes with very little improvisation. Corporate event planners don't like surprises."

Cezar is adamant that the most important thing that an aspiring band or DJ can do to gain success in the industry is to be on time, be professional, and be consistently good. He spent years as an agent, often dealing with problem performers. "It was discouraging as an agent to deal with people who were always late, or sometimes would just not show up. It was incredible to me that this went on at first, but I learned that that's just the way that some people operate." He notes that if you want to be successful, put the client first and your hard work will be appreciated. This will translate into more work in the future.

For bands, Cezar explains that the responsibilities are usually split among the band members. "One person is responsible for the overall setting up of the stage. We all take care of our own instruments, but one person should have final say on the mixer, the P.A., and the cables, et cetera." Cezar notes that the person should be technically sound and have an interest in it. Two other band members might take the duty of setting up the lights, for example. The drummer sets up their drums. Maybe you have a sound guy, or else those duties fall to one of the members of the band.

"I personally handle all of the business dealings with the band— booking the gigs and handling the finances," he notes. He splits out the website responsibilities, like making sure that the web content is current, that the links work, and that emails and inquiries are handled promptly.

20/20 is a great example of a band who survived and thrived by playing countless corporate gigs in and around the Calgary area—and Cezar grew the business over his twenty-plus years to include several exciting national events as well.

Appendix 2:
Case Study – Jim Casey
Entertainment

"I had a mobile DJ friend who gave me a chance to assist a couple of times at a wedding. On April 12, 1997, I performed my first wedding reception at a pit of a facility called Paul Junior's Hall in Lewiston, Maine for a massive pay day of $175." With that start, Jim Casey Entertainment began his run at becoming a successful DJ in the Maine area.

"I got my start in 1985 as a Board Operator for a small AM Radio station in Portland, Maine. From there, I worked my way through 15 different AM and FM stations in 12 years, getting fired from nearly all of them," Jim laughs.

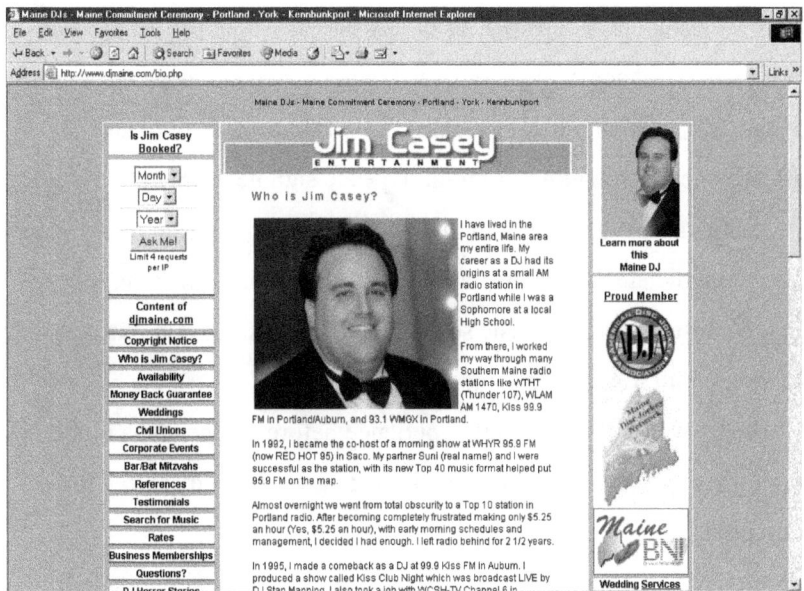

Jim Casey's earlier website showed a sense of humor but was quite detailed and professional.

"Then, in 1996, as I was ending a two year run of a popular Saturday night show called 'Kiss Club Night at the Portland Ramada', I was approached by a mother of the bride asking me if I would do her daughter's wedding. I found this amusing since I had been married only a few short months before, but said I would give it a shot.

"The reception was three weeks after the wedding itself. The groom was dressed in a shirt and tie, the bride showed up in sweatpants and a t-shirt. I did five more weddings that year and figured out I was pretty good at them."

Jim Casey offers DJ services for a variety of events, including weddings and corporate gigs. However, his knowledge in the industry has enabled him to expand out. His website offers party supplies, such as glow bracelets, necklaces, and a multitude of birthday party items. These items are valuable at staff parties or any events where people can win door prizes, a dance contest, or even just receive them as party favors or giveaways. You can book Jim Casey for a DJ event, or purchase inflatable feet and a glow-in-the-dark peace sign necklace.

Like many other DJs, Jim knows that personal taste in music alone should not dictate what gets played at an event. "I try never to let my personal taste sway my music selections. I like a lot of pop music, top 40, along with R&B, disco, and Sinatra."

With over a decade of DJ experience before he became a mobile DJ, Jim knows that professionalism and a strong work ethic are key to succeeding.

"A professional Disc Jockey must at all times be as positive in their presentation as possible," he notes. "It will show in every aspect of the business, from prospect meetings, to pre-wedding consultations, to performances. Most talent in this business can be learned, but a great and positive personality is inherent. Truthfully, to do this profession correctly, you must be willing to go the extra mile for your clients. Hitting a few buttons on a CD player or computer can be done by anybody. The truly talented people in our profession are the best listeners. They will listen to their client's needs and assist them in the best ways to represent that during their special event, whether it is a wedding reception, bar or bat mitzvah, et cetera."

What type of person is best suited to become a DJ? While some are introverted, quiet people who hide behind their equipment, and others are outgoing, loud and the center of attention, Jim admits that he falls somewhere in the middle.

"I am a very complicated person. When I am at an event for instance, I am very out-going, confident (but not cocky) in every way. I am in control of the environment while remaining a team player with the photographers, catering staff and the facility coordinators.

"Once I am finished, I become a fairly quiet and introverted person until I know someone. People within my inner circle would probably describe me as brash, sometimes obnoxious, but willing to tell it like it is. They would also say I am very helpful when people have problems."

Jim Casey uses a 10x6 cube that houses his personal computer, a Numark Dual CD+G Player, a Numark Mixing Board, two Sennheisser Wireless Microphones, and an 15" LCD Monitor. "The only speakers I use are 2 12" FBT Maxx 4a Powered Speakers. Before this, I simply used a Numark CD Mix 2 and the two powered speakers. By the way, my approach is a heck of a lot different than most. I have never used a Sub Woofer in my 9 plus years as a mobile. I haven't truthfully seen the need for one."

There are many great events that stand out in Jim Casey's mind, but he shares a few memorable experiences that have fueled his desire to keep spinning tunes.

"Picking favorite gigs is like selecting your favorite children. In April 2006, I did my second wedding with the same family. The first was in December 2004 at a very high end facility on the coast of Maine. Everything that night was perfect. People were happy because of the nearing holidays and they were in the mood to party.

"The dance floor was filled for the entire evening. At the end of that night, I had four separate people come up to me and tip me. I was stunned to later see $180 in my pocket.

"Expectations were very high for the follow-up event and I was admittedly quite nervous about this. One thing I had going for me is that I did things slightly different than before. I was a bit more daring as an emcee without taking over the event. I approached people during the cocktail/social hour to get music requests. It broke that barrier that people sometimes feel. I couldn't pick a bad song.

Jim notes that the effort he gave to be social paid off. "At the end of the night, two people gave me tips. This time, I had $120."

Jim Casey Entertainment, like many DJs, have embraced the digital age and uses computer files when DJing. However, he is quick to note that he employs a backup strategy.

"I have been digital since June 2005 with no regrets. However, I always carry my CDs as backup just in case the unthinkable occurs. Backup plans are probably a DJs number one weapon to combat failure."

Jim Casey exudes confidence and personality. He offers a "7-point guarantee" for his clients, which places professionalism and peace of mind in the client's head when they are searching for a DJ. It includes a "proper attire" guarantee, an "event planning" guarantee and a "coordination with other professionals" guarantee to help put the client at ease. If that wasn't enough, he also has a "DJ horror stories" section on his website that offers up nightmares that other DJ clients have had to endure because they chose another DJ... one that was definitely not Jim Casey.

2009 was a year of transition for Jim, as he moved from Maine to sunny Florida and set up shop down south. Despite the new location and clientele, Jim uses the same equipment for DJing.

"As for equipment, I use a Numark CD Mix 2 in a modified case that holds my sound card and two wireless microphone sets. The Mix 2 is hooked to my 2 FBT Powered Speakers."

Jim was excited about the move to Florida. "I have always disliked the snow and cold," explains Jim. "Maine is very unfriendly as far as a business climate and high taxes go. Plus, my family and I had been vacationing in Florida several times per winter. After one of those trips, we decided to take a leap of faith and prepare to move." The move involved some life changes and planning, just like running a business. "We aggressively sold our home, and I stopped taking new bookings. My wife needed to find a new job in Florida before we could move." Despite the hard work, Jim is happy with the decision. "No income taxes, and warmer climate equals better business opportunities," he says.

Jim has had an extremely busy year with non-stop bookings and gigs. "I believe that since I have been able to expand what I offer, it has allowed me to continue to be successful. Stagnation in this type of work will kill your business."

Jim Casey's website, like his business, continues to grow—note the slick social media tags (Facebook, Twitter, etc) in the top-right corner.

Appendix 3:
Wedding Checklist

For most DJs, weddings are either going to rank among your favorite gigs or they will be the most time-consuming and frustrating. Often they are both. As the DJ, you are dealing with a wedding couple's most important, high-profile day of their lives. Of course, it is an incredibly special day for the entire family, and everyone it seems is an expert when it comes to the music.

A successful DJ will not only play the appropriate music, but will make the client aware that they will play the appropriate music. It's not enough to just be good; you also have to communicate that with the customer. In many cases, you need to put their mind at ease.

How do you make the customer happy? The first and foremost skill that every great DJ needs is to listen. Make sure that you are aware of the client's needs and wants. If you are not able to provide what they are looking for, be up front and honest and tell them. They may shrug their shoulders and say "no big deal" and work out an alternate arrangement that suits them (and you) just fine. Remember, no one is forcing you to take the gig!

Usually the bride and groom will have very specific songs that they want played. I usually just ask them for those songs and then, if I don't have them, they almost always offer to provide a CD with their songs on it. The other option is that they just e-mail me the mp3 files so I can play the songs that they want to hear.

Sometimes the best way to see what is important to the bride and groom is to check out wedding planning websites. These usually offer "things to ask" or "things to research" for people who are looking to plan their own wedding. Remember, these tips below are not from DJ websites or companies; they are from wedding planners. Read these tips from the viewpoint of the consumer.

Music: What is the DJs policy on requests? Is there anything available for your customers to look at regarding songs or artists? Your wedding will most likely feature music that will satisfy all ages (children, adults and seniors). Ask about the available variety of genres and the approximate number of songs at the DJ's disposal. Also, ask your DJ how familiar he is with the genre of music that you would like played.

Equipment: How professional and solid is the DJ gear? A professional DJ should not be using "home" gear such as a CD player and home stereo system.

Extras: Are lighting, games and fog important to you? What about contests or other special promotions or events during your wedding reception? Ask about what (if any) are included in your package.

Attitude: A professional DJ will sit down with you and explain the details of the wedding reception. This includes going over the toasts, emceeing duties, first dance, blessings and prayers (if any), cake cutting, bouquet and garter toss, and any special requested stoppages in the proceedings or dances. They should be able to listen to you and your ideas and meet any special needs that you have.

Experience: Does your DJ have references? They should be able to provide you with at least three clients that they have previously worked with. Try to determine if the DJ has the experience you need. Are they able to "read a crowd" and even motivate them to dance if the room goes quiet?

You might want to check out your DJ if they play at a local nightclub or bar so you can see him or her in action before you decide to sign a contract. Alternatively, ask if there is a videotape or digital clip of the DJ in action so you can judge for yourself.

Remember, the food and the music are the most important parts of the wedding reception. Make sure that you have all the bases covered.

Appendix 4:
Freeware & Low Cost Stuff

I was at a meeting recently with some friends who were thinking about buying a condo. We wanted to buy a place in Hawaii and rent it out. It would also be a great place to vacation every now and then. Of course, as a group we were interested in having a really nice place, but we were not interested in buying things for the condo that would either be destroyed or stolen. It was also important that we were buying things for the condo with the idea that everything in the condo was *designed to increase the value of the service provided to the client.*

Think about that last sentence for a minute. Why would you buy super-high-end towels for your bathroom if your clients, who are paying you money, aren't going to care? What is important to the client? A second or third bedroom? High-end towels? Basic cable, or a movie channel? A plasma or big-screen LCD TV? High-speed internet?

This same question is at the heart of pretty much every business that is out there. Imagine a bakery. The baker is going to use high-quality ingredients, but only to the point that the client cares. He's not going to spend $200 on a bag of super-fancy flour if the client wants a loaf of bread for ninety-nine cents!

I say this because one of the biggest mistakes that you can make starting out as a DJ is blowing your bank on unnecessary items that will not help you make money. For example, there is DJ software out there for $800 that will help you create your own music. You can mash up, remix, re-cut, and publish your own music. Wow! That is great, but will spending the $800 on that product help you get any paying gigs? I am guessing, at least at the start anyway, that the answer in many cases is a resounding "no".

The same is true with smoke machines, huge disco balls, a super-expensive website, plastic skeletons, Christmas decorations, a $900 three-piece suit, or television advertising. Some of these items, or none of these items may be what you are looking for. But you must make sure that if you do purchase any item, it is because you are doing so with the goal of increasing your sales. Without sales, you don't have a business—you just have a hobby.

The following are just some suggestions of low-cost and free items that you can use when starting up a company. (Nobody has paid any money to appear here and I cannot guarantee that every one of these items is perfect. Try them out and see if they work for you.)

Audio Freeware

- VU Player: This lightweight audio player is freeware. This means that you can download it, use it, share it—the software is completely free and legally available. Visit www.vuplayer.com for details.
- KraMixer is an audio player that boasts an intuitive layout and even the ability to record mixes. Check out www.kramware.com.
- Audacity is free, open-source editing software. It is found at http://audacity.sourceforge.net/. It is a little less user-friendly than a simple "point and click" software but once you get the hang of it, you can cut and paste, add in effects, and play around with mp3 files.

- Mixxx is free software that is also open source, meaning that anyone can download the software and modify it. It is completely free and is found at www.mixxx.org. They boast a myriad of features such a multichannel support, extra skins (in effect you can change the appearance of the player on your computer screen) and adjustable equalizer shelves.

- Mixvibes is a simple, two-turntable interface that lets you load up one track while playing another. You can also cross fade from one track to another. Check out www.freewarefiles.com/MixVibes-Free_program_12243.html to download it or www.mixvibes.com for the full website.

- iTunes Store: if you are using an iPad or iPod, simply go the iTunes store (or google "free apps DJ" and search through the options. I recommend trying for free first before purchasing. There is a huge variety in the quality of apps—some are quite professional, while some users may find some low-end apps not suitable for DJing at the professional level.

Website

Designing your own website can be fun and exciting, or it can be an expensive pain. Here are some free and low-cost ideas for hosting a website.

www.bravenet.com has both a free and professional list of services. If you want a free website, it does not get much easier than this. If you want free, be prepared to have either advertising on your website (ads that you do not control), or your domain name may not be exactly what you wanted (for example, if you want www.happydj.com, you might wind up with www.bravenet.com/happydj instead). If you purchase the services, you can get a website domain name, multiple templates to use in order to set up a website without learning html code, and other tools that can help you and your clients see what services you offer.

- www.110mb.com claims that you can have a website up and running in 5 minutes! They offer, as the name suggests, 110 MB of space, a template site builder and Shockwave & Flash support.

- www.facebook.com is one of the most popular sites in the world, and it is free. You can set up a personal page, and then also connect with other people around the world. Try setting up a professional DJ page if you want to include photos and testimonies of events that you have worked.

- www.twitter.com is a very popular social networking site. Set up your business and make sure to consistently send out fun tweets to your followers.

- www.blogger.com is a hugely popular blogging website, powered by Google. You can get a free blog by signing up, although the domain name will be in the form of "your business" and then "blogspot.com" in the title. Blogs can be a fun way to update the world about your business and help create buzz regarding songs, software and business. Your blog could be about weddings, for example, and you could describe different DJ gigs that have a common theme. Someone googling "wedding DJs" could stumble across your blog and read all about your business exploits. Make sure to have your contact information handy on the blog in the event that a potential client needs to get a hold of you.

As with any business idea, these websites and social media

functions won't run themselves. Make sure to actively keep your website fresh, professional (for example, make sure your links work) and keep it fun!

Index

ABOUT THE AUTHOR

Karl Wiebe is a Canadian author who calls Calgary his home. Originally born in Toronto, his family moved out to Calgary where he found a passion for writing while in junior high school. Karl graduated from university with a Bachelor's Degree in General Management from the Faculty of Business at Lakehead University in Thunder Bay, Ontario.

Karl eventually moved back to Calgary and began to DJ, finding a profitable niche in the classic rock genre. He has deejayed for over seven years, playing numerous weddings, community hall parties, and even an awards banquet for the Calgary Hitmen hockey team. One of the highlights of his musical career was playing a banquet for contest winners at a Def Leppard concert – let's get rocked!

Karl's favorite music includes U2, Dire Straits, The Beatles, Green Day, Jack White and KISS—although any music that will empty the seats and get people out on the dance floor is alright with him!

Check out www.karlwiebe.com for more information about books and projects.